H. Wren

The Fall of Babylon

H. Wren

The Fall of Babylon

ISBN/EAN: 9783337240431

Printed in Europe, USA, Canada, Australia, Japan

Cover: Foto ©ninafisch / pixelio.de

More available books at **www.hansebooks.com**

—⊢·THE·⊣—

FALL OF BABYLON,

AND

THE LOUD CRY.

BY

H. WREN. A. M.

PART FIRST.

THE FALL OF BABYLON.

"And after these things I saw another angel come down from heaven, having great power, and the earth was lightened with his glory. And he cried mightily, with a strong voice, saying, 'Babylon, the great, is fallen, is fallen;' and is become the habitation of devils, and the hold of every foul spirit, and a cage of every unclean and hateful bird. And I heard another voice from heaven, saying, 'Come out of her, my people, that ye be not partakers of her sins, and that ye receive not of her plagues. For her sins have reached unto heaven, and God hath remembered her iniquities.'"—Rev. 18, 1—5.

This tract is an old fashioned believer in the Bible. It is addressed to those who fear the God therein revealed, and think its sayings worthy to be kept. It undertakes to break new ground in the field covered by the pages of the Sacred Book.

It will attempt an exposition of the eighteenth chapter of Revelation. This will involve a review of the entire work of God, and history of the world, from a new stand-point, as the light which the mighty angel there described sheds over the world is but the sum of all the rays of light which, from age to age, have fallen upon men; while the sins there attributed to Babylon are but the sins of all the ages past reduced into a living mass of existing evil. The sins of this Babylon are the last great cloud to darken the skies of earth, while the light of that angel is a burst of the sun of divine Revelation, full-orbed, upon a fallen world, as that sun sets to rise no more.

That the work of this angel is the closing work of the Gospel dispensation, and that the time for it has fully come, will be amply proven, on the pages of this tract to those who have a knowledge of the great system of prophesy, as spread out on the pages of the Bible. To those who are not familiar with this portion of Scripture, we wish to say, that we have made many statements which we have not undertaken to prove—since our object is not so much to write an exposition of prophesy as to call your attention to expositions that have already been made and placed before the world. By these statements we desire to stir you up to an investigation of the truthfulness of our assertions, believing that such an inquiry will lead you to see the matter in the same light. There is not a statement in the tract but we hold ourselves ready to make good, upon evidence which must elicit the confidence of the candid. But if our statements are not true, any of the ministry of our day can show them to be wrong, or erroneous. So that the inquiry we desire you to make in the premises can only result in an increase of knowledge, one way or the other. And therefore, we earnestly invite your attention to the matters brought forward by these pages We are now ready to take up our subject, and we first invite your attention to the

THE MIGHTY ANGEL.

John saw coming down from heaven, and whose glory, he declares, enlightened the earth. What is this angel? Is it a literal angel? Or is it a man, or a body of men, symbolized by an angel? We think it is the latter. It appears to us to be the ministry of the church, at the time referred to. But does some one ask—"did not a literal angel warn Abraham of the impending fate of Sodom? Did not literal angels summon Lot to make haste and escape for his life? Did not literal angels sing "glory to God in the highest" to the Shepherds at our Savior's birth? And are not all the literal "angels ministering spirits sent sent forth to minister to those who shall be the beirs.of Salvation?" And may not this be a literal angel?

We acknowledge that we are happy to believe that all the above and much more is true of the literal angels., For, without the assistance of the literal angels, we fear that the service of the symbolic angels would not come to much. Still, we think, this angel is symbolic. We think there are two tests that will solve the question, in every case, whether a given angel is to be regarded as literal, or symbolic. It is to be regarded as symbolic. First, when it is doing a work in reference to the general mass of mankind, or in behalf of the general body of God's people. Second, when that work is evident by a proclamation of the Gospel. These tests are in the case of the angels of the seven churches of Rev. 2 and 3, and in the case of the three angels of Rev. 14: 6—12. These all are, therefore, evidently, symbolic angels, or the ministers of Christ, represented by that name. Still more obviously, if possible, do both these tests meet in our angel of Rev. 18. His work relates to the mass of God's people and also to the world. And it is manifestly a proclamation of the Gospel for it exposes, by its light, the sins that are current in its day, and throws its radiance over the pathway of the children of God, as they retire from Babylon. Having thus introduced "the hero of our story," we now venture to assert, that, the work attributed to him, in the chapter we are considering,

HAS NOT YET BEEN DONE.

We believe this for the following reasons : First. No one has ever claimed to be doing it. Neither Luther, Calvin, Wesley, nor any other of the great lights of modern times, set up the claim that he was doing this work. But, if it had been done by any of them, they would have known it. For while it is true that wicked men and nations fulfill the word of God without knowing it, this is not the case with God's people. Whenever men are raised up by God among his people to do a work that had been foretold in the Bible, those men know that they are fulfilling prophesy. And they know the very prophesy which is being wrought out through them. John, the Baptist, knew that he was the one foretold by Isaiah, as "crying in the wilderness, prepare ye the way of the Lord." The great reformers knew that they were raised up to break the dominion of the papacy over the consciences of men, as had been foretold would be done. The leaders in the great Advent movements of the present century knew that they were proclaiming the messages described as being given by three angels in Rev. 14: 6–12. Now this work of the angel of Rev. 18, is a specific work among God's people and in their behalf. Hence, if it ever had been done, his servants who did it would have known it, and left the mark and record of their work in the world. But there is no people who trace their origin to the fulfillment of this prophesy, nor any record to show that anybody ever claimed to be engaged in the work here described. We conclude, therefore, that it has not been done. As a further proof that this angel has not yet done his work we mention,

Second. Babylon has never been in the condition ascribed to her by this angel until now. And therefore this work could not have been done heretofore. The truth of this will become more and more apparent as we proceed with the subject. As a final reason for insisting that this work is not yet accomplished, we mention, Third. That, if it had been done the world would have ended ere this; Because the pouring out of the "plagues," the overthrow of Babylon, and the destruction of the world immediately follow it. Read the entire chapter, and the remainder of the book of Revelation, and see if this is not the case. But, if we understand the situation, the plagues are not yet poured out, Babylon is not yet overthrown, and the wicked are not yet destroyed. Hence, again, we conclude that the work of this angel is not yet done. But we are prepared to lay down the proposition that

IT IS NOW DUE.

The time has come for its glory to lighten the earth. The evidence in proof of this is found in fact, as can be easily proven, though we do not here try to prove it—that nearly every event foretold in the Bible to precede the end of the world and the Day of God's Wrath, except this angel work, and the events to arise out of, and in connection with it, has taken place, and is now in the past. The rise and fall of mighty kingdoms in past ages; the character and origin of the political powers now upon the scene of action; the appearance of great ecclesiastical bodies and the work they would do in this and past ages; the development of the great schemes of Satan, from age to age, and their culmination at this time, by which he would subvert or overthrow the work of God in the earth; the steady and onward march of the work of Christ towards its final and triumphant conclusion, all show that time can last but little longer, and set us on the alert for any tokens there may be of the approach of that angel which is to lend the lustre of his glory to the earth for a brief space at the close of its history.

In special confirmation of our belief that the hour this angel's work has come, we mention one fact : It has already been shown, that the work of this angel immediately precedes the falling of the last plagues, and the end of the world. By reading what is said of the "Third Angel," and the events directly following it, as shown in the latter part of Rev. 14, it will be also seen, that the coming of the Lord in the clouds of heaven and the end of the world immediately follow the work of that angel. Hence—as God does not have two special forms of Gospel work going on at the same time, we conclude, that the "Third Angel" of Rev. 14, and the angel of Rev. 18, are the same, and represent the same work substantially. The angel of Rev. 18, doubtless has a special work of its own, in the doing of which it absorbs and continues the work of the "Third Angel" of Rev. 14. And quickly gathers the people of God into one body, prepares them for translation and brings to a glorious issue the militant history of the church of Jesus Christ. The significant fact that we now state is : That the work of the "Third Angel" of Rev. 14, has been going on in the earth for over forty years. If any candid person should doubt this, let him call and get the proof. It is ready and ample. It must be, therefore, that the stage of the work described in Rev. 14, is far advanced. Whenever that angel begirts the earth with his work, the time will be arrived for the opening of Rev. 18. But the "Third Angel," at this day, encircles the earth. The hour for the "mighty Angel" of Rev. 18, is, therefore, at hand. If the above views are correct, and we are sure they are—The Seventh Day Adventists have given the message of Rev. 14, referred to above, and the work of the angel of Rev. 18, must be expected to arise among that people. It is now a matter of interest to inquire.

WHAT IS BABYLON ?

And where shall we look to find it? It is not necessary to say that it is not literal Babylon, or the ancient city of Asia, once bearing that name. She is no more. Her pride and sins brought her downfall long ago. The Babylon of which we are now speaking must be some other. We have seen that the angel of whose work we are writing was a symbolic angel. It is not unlikely then, that this is a symbolic Babylon. We believe it is. There evidently are several Babylons mentioned in the Bible. But there never has been but one actual, or literal, Babylon. The first, or literal, Babylon was the product, in the first instance, and afterward, the chief stay and propagator of idolatry, or the first great apostasy of men from God. Ancient Babylon was the centre and glory of Paganism. Now, how reasonable—if there should be a second great apostasy, even if it differed materially, from the first, it would be to call it by the same name. And this is just what is done in the book of Revelation. The second apostasy is the apostasy of the Christian world from revealed and restored truth, just as the first or pagan apostasy was from the original truth given man at his creation. The entire Christian world, in so far as it is, ever has been, or will be, apostate, is included in the various instances in which Babylon is referred to in the book of Revelation. Before this tract is finished, we shall place before you the most conclusive proof that, not only the church of Rome, the Greek Church of Russia, and other State Churches, are in a state of apostasy, but that this is also the condition of all the great Protestant bodies of our day. But we wish to state our belief, here, that while this Babylon of Rev. 18 takes in the entire Christian world, almost, it is our Protestant churches that are chiefly meant. This will appear when we observe the fact, that this Babylon is not declared fallen until just before the end of the world. It must therefore chiefly embrace that part of the Christian world which apostatizes near the close of time. We, therefore, conclude that this is not ancient, and literal, but modern, and symbolic Babylon, or the Christian world of our day. We now propose to bring forward proof that every candid man will recognize as conclusive, that,

BABYLON IS FALLEN.

We spread before you what one of the ablest and most eloquent bishops of the M. E. Church says of his own denomination. Here is his language : "The Church of God is to-day courting the world. Its members are trying to bring it down to the level of the ungodly. The ball, the theatre, nude and lewd art, social luxuries, with all their loose immoralities, are making inroads into the sacred inclosure of the Church. And as a satisfaction for all this worldliness, Christians are making a great deal of Lent and Easter and Good Friday, and church ornamentation. It is the old trick of Satan. The Jewish Church struck on that rock. The Romish Church was wrecked on the same. And the Protestant Church is fast reaching the same doom.

Our great dangers, as we see them, are, assimilation to the world, neglect of the poor, substitution of the form for the fact of Godliness, abandonment of discipline, a hireling ministry, an impure gospel; which, summed up, is a fashionable church. That Methodists should be liable to such an outcome, and that there should be signs of it in a hundred years from the sail-loft, seems almost the miracle of history. But who that looks about him to-day can fail to see the fact.

Do not Methodists, in violation of God's word and their own discipline, dress as extravagantly and as fashionably as any other class? Do not the ladies, and often the wives and daughters of the ministry, put on gold and pearls, and costly array? Would not the plain dress insisted on by John Wesley, Bishop Asbury, and worn by Hester Ann Rogers, lady Huntington, and others equally distinguished, be now regarded in Methodist circles as fanaticism? Can any one. going into a Methodist Church in any of our chief cities, distinguish the attire of the communicants from that of the theatre and ball goers?

Is not worldliness seen in the music? Elaborately dressed and ornamented choirs, who in many cases make no profession of religion, and are often sneering skeptics, go through a cold, artistic, or operatic performance, which is as much in harmony with spiritual worship as an opera, or theatre. Under such wordly performances spirituality is frozen to death.

Formerly every Methodist attended class and gave testimony of experimental religion. Now the class meeting is attended by very few, and in many churches abandoned. Seldom the stewards, trustees and leaders attend class. Formerly nearly every Methodist prayed. testified or exhorted in prayer meeting. Now but few are heard. Formerly shouts and praises were heard. Now such demonstrations of holy enthusiasm and joy are regarded as fanaticism.

Worldly socials, fairs, festivals, concerts and such like have taken the place of the religious gatherings, revival meetings, class and prayer meetings of earlier days. How true that the Methodist Discipline is a dead letter. Its rules forbid the wearing of gold, or pearls, or costly array. Yet no one ever thinks of disciplining its members for violating them. They forbid the reading of such books, and the taking of such diversions as do not minister to godliness. Yet the church itself goes to shows and frolics, and fairs, which destroy the spiritual life of the young, as well as the old. The extent to which this is now carried on is appalling. The spiritual death it carries in its train will only be known when the millions it has swept into hell stand before the judgment.

The early Methodist ministers went out to sacrifice and suffer for Christ. They sought not place of ease and affluence, but of privation and suffering. They gloried not in their big salaries, fine parsonages. and refined congregations, but in the souls that had been won for Jesus. Oh, how changed! A hireling ministry will be a feeble, a timid, a truckling, a time serving ministry, without faith, endurance and holy power. Methodism formerly dealt in the great central truth. Now the pulpits deal largely in generalities and in popular lectures. The glorious doctrine of entire sanctification is rarely heard or seldom witnessed to in the pulpits."

These are the charges that one of her foremost bishops makes against the M. E. Church. Has he overdrawn the picture? It is not likely that he has. It is much more likely that his description falls below the truth. His language is not that of a man wreaking vengeance on his church for some neglect, or wrong, it has shown him, and to this end calls to his assistance the language of vituperation and calumny. But, on the other hand. it is the language of a man actually in the enjoyment of the highest honor his church can bestow upon him; and who. therefore, would never have spoken such words of his church. unless he had felt driven to it by the most solemn convictions of duty: and then his love for, and his pride in his church would dictate to him to use the most moderate language that would at all answer. Has not this Bishop truly given us the picture of a fallen church? If he has not how could it be done? If a church in which worldliness has taken the place of spirituality; fairs and festivals. the place of religious meetings; a time serving and feeble ministry, the place of a self-denying ministry; and if a church in which the word of God, as well as its own discipline, is violated with impunity is not a fallen church, please tell us what would constitute a fallen church.

But the above does not apply exclusively to the church of which it was chiefly spoken. It is a picture of the state of things existing nearly everywhere among the churches of our day. Does not everybody know that such is the fact? Who would assert the contrary? "Babylon is fallen, is fallen." We shall now take up a question, in connection with the fallen condition of the religious world, in regard to which the Bishop quoted above is silent. The question to which we refer is,—

WHAT IS THE 'CAUSE

of the existing state of things? Why are the churches in this deplorable condition? Were they always so? Or is this a recent matter? They were not always in this state? For the Bishop quoted in the former chapter compares the present condition of his denomination with its former state, and shows that there has been a great change from the better to the worse—in fact, from the good to the bad. There must have been some event, or factor, in the history of these churches that has separated them from God, and as a result of such separation, the existing state of things has, either wholly come about, or been greatly increased. We shall here take the position that the underlying cause of the fallen condition of the Christian world is to be found in

THE REJECTION OF TRUTH.

The churches of our day have rejected great light from the word and providence of God. We shall proceed to enumerate the leading features of divine truth which are set at naught by the religious world at this time. We, therefore, ask your serious and candid attention to what follows: The first special charge of this kind we make against the Christian world is, that they reject light in regard to the

SECOND COMING OF CHRIST.

During the last fifty years the world has been flooded with light, full and ample in regard to this event. Nearly every event foretold in the word of God to precede his coming has been shown to have transpired. It has been shown, that the Gospel is now preached among all nations, as our Lord said in Matt. 24: 14, would be the case just before the end. It has been shown that iniquity abounds as Jesus said in Matt. 24:13, and as Paul said in 2 Tim. 3: 1—5. would be the case in the last days. It has been shown that Spiritualism is the work of Satan and fallen angels, working miracles and deceiving the world in "the latter time," and just before the end of the world; as had been foretold in 2 Thess. 2:9, 1 Tim. 4:1, Rev. 14:16 and other places. It has been shown that the nations are now disturbed and perplexed, men's hearts failing them for fear as they look for some great evil to come upon the earth; as is foretold in Luke 21:26, will be the case just before the Lord is seen coming in the clouds of heaven. It has been shown that the sun and moon have been darkened, and the stars fallen, as was foretold in Matt. 24:29, Luke 21:25, and Rev. 6:12, 13, would be the case, when the heavens are about to pass away, and the day of wrath about to break upon the inhabitants of the earth.

Furthermore, it has been well and truly proven, that nearly every event foreshadowed by the great system of symbolic prophesy has taken place. To specify somewhat, we will assert, that it has been proven, that the great Image of Dan. 2, represents the world's history, in outline, from the Noachian deluge to the second coming of Christ; and that the only event yet to transpire in its history, is its destruction by collision with the little stone, or the second advent of Jesus Christ. In regard to the symbols of Dan. 7, it has been shown that the four beasts there described represent the history of the world down to the last great judgment, as is seen from reading the first ten verses. in the last two of which Daniel says—"I beheld till the thrones were cast down and the Ancient of Days did sit, whose garment was white as snow, and the hair of his head like pure wool. His throne was like the fiery flame, and his wheels as burning fire. A fiery stream issued and came forth from before him. Thousand thousands ministered unto him, and ten thousand times ten thousand stood before him. The judgment was set and the books were opened." It has been shown that the "little horn" of the fourth beast represents the papacy; and that at the time its dominion is taken away the judgment shall sit: as is seen by reading verse 26. But the dominion of the Papacy has been shown to be taken away at this day; and therefore it has been insisted, that the time for the last great judgment has arrived. In regard to Dan. 8, it has been shown that all the events there described have taken place. It has been proven that the twenty-three hundred days of verse 14 are years, and that they are in the past. Attention has been called to the fact that the Cleansing of the Sanctuary, or the judgment of the last day, was to occur at their termination, and that therefore this work must be at hand. The events foretold in Dan. 11 and 12 have been shown to be passed. except the "standing up of Michael," and "the time of trouble," and that for this reason the day of wrath is near.

Passing the stately pages of Daniel, we enter the more graphic and thrilling scenes spread out in book of Revelation. And, taking things in the order in which they come before us, we notice the letters to be seven churches, as found in chapters 2 and 3. and assert that it has been clearly proven, that they represent seven different stages of the history of the church. from the Apostolic age to the close of time: and that it has been shown that we are now living in the last, or Laodicean stage of that history: and that we must believe, for this reason, that the end is not far off. The seven seals have been taken up and expounded and it has been shown that we are living under the last events of the sixth seal, and that therefore, the heavens are about to pass away, and the day of wrath fully break upon the world. The Seven Trumpets of chapters 8 and 9, have been shown to represent the great wars that the northern barbarians, and after them. the great Mahomet and his successors, waged in Europe and Asia; as well as the history of European Turkey. It has been shown that we are now living under the seventh of these trumpets. and that the "mystery of God," or the work of the gospel, is about to be finished, in harmony with Rev. 10:7: and that therefore, we are not far from the end. In regard to chapter 10 it has been shown that it met its fulfillment in the great Advent Movement under William Miller and in the disappointment in which it ended. The events of Rev. 11 have been proven to be chiefly in the past. and that the time mentioned in verse 18. that the "dead should be judged" is at hand. and that for this reason "the kingdoms of this world are about to be given to our God and to his Christ." The events represented by the history of the great red dragon. and the woman clothed with the sun, in Rev. 12, took place. as has been shown in the persecution of God's people for ages. at the hand of Rome. and that we are now in the time foretold in verse 17. where the remnant of the woman's seed. on the last generation of the people of God. are to appear upon the stage of the world. having "the commandments of God and the faith of Jesus" in their possession. on account of which they are to experience a last and final conflict with the dragon. For this reason it has been again insisted, that the end is near at hand. In regard to the first beast of Rev. 13, it has been shown that it represents the Papacy down to the year A. D., 1798.

Attention has been called to the fact, that just at this point, John not only drops the history of the first beast, but brings forward another, which he describes as "having horns like a lamb." It has been shown that this second beast represents the United States which was just rising into prominence among the nations in 1798. It has been proven that Sunday is the mark of the beast. It has been shown that there is now on foot in this country a great movement known as "The National Reform" Movement; having for its object to secure more stringent legislation in support of Sunday. It has been shown that the current in this direction is so strong, that it is only a matter of time when that movement will eventuate in the most rigorous persecution. and the Protestant world repeat the history of Rome, as is foretold will be the case in closing events of history. In view of this matter also it has been held that we are near the close of time. In concluding this list of facts, going to show, that the second coming of Christ is near at hand, we state, that it has been proven that the great messages described in Rev. 14: 6—12, as being given by three angels, have been heard in the world, in the great Advent movements of the present generation, and that we are now about to witness the conclusion of their work, in the proclamation of the mighty angel of Rev. 18. This fact again shows, as has been insisted upon, that the Lord is soon to appear.

Thus has the proof been given, that the second coming of our Lord Jesus Christ is at hand. Proof drawn from prophesy, drawn from history, drawn from the present state of the world, drawn from the state of the churches, drawn from the progress of the plan of redemption, in heaven and on earth, drawn from the sun and moon, and from the stars of light. Thus it is seen that nature, "through all her elements," unites with all nations, and churches, and with God, angels, demons and men, to proclaim to the inhabitants of earth, that "The Great Day" is at hand.

But what has the Christian world done with all this array of proof ? Have they accepted it, as if they wished to show their faith in, and love for, the word of God? No. They have rejected it with disgust and abhorrence. And on what ground have they rejected it? Is it because they have opened their Bibles, and the history of the world, and shown these interpretations to be wrong? Have they gone through what our Savior and Paul said would transpire in the last days, and shown, that those things have not yet come to pass, and that therefore, we are not near the end? If they have done this, where is the record to show they did it? Have they reviewed the great field of symbolic prophesy, as given in the books of Daniel and Revelation, and shown that the events covered by those symbols have not yet come to pass, and that therefore, the end is not near? If they have done this, we should be glad to learn when and where they did it. Have they shown that the various lines of events called for by the seven letters, the seven seals, and the seven trumpets, have not been developed, and that therefore, we should not expect the end soon? If they have done this, when, where and how did they do it? Have they shown that the messages proclaimed by the three angels described in Rev. 14, have not been placed before the present inhabitants of earth, and that therefore, the coming of our Lord is not near at hand? It would greatly please us to know at what time and place, and by what means, they did this. Have the leaders of the Christian world rejected the coming of the Lord, and the vast mass of evidence in proof of it, for such reasons as the foregoing? No. But they reject it because—because—because—Mr. Miller made a mistake, some people sold their property, some others neglected theirs, and some were actually reported to have put on ascension robes ! ! !

Thus the matter stands, and thus it will stand when the Christian world is summoned before the great white throne to answer for its conduct in the premises; unless its leaders can arrest the progress of the car of Providence, by throwing across its track their fancied millennium. But we anticipate that the ponderous wheels of that car will move resistlessly on, over both them and their beloved millenninm, towards the goal of a speedy and glorious destiny. We next charge upon the leaders, and the great mass of the Christian world, that they reject light in regard to the doctrine of

IMMORTALITY.

Great light has been shed abroad in our day on this subject. It has been shown that God alone is the great reservoir of immorality; as is declared in 1 Tim. 6:17. And that from this original source it is imparted to those "who by patient continuance in well doing, seek for glory, and honor, and immorality," in harmony with Rom. 2:7. It has been also shown from the same connection, that it is "rendered" to such at the day of judgment. It has been shown from 1 Cor. 15: 51—58 that the righteous "put on immortality" at the resurrection. It has been insisted that in view of the preceding, and other scriptures, it cannot be true, that immortality is a natural gift, inherited, or bestowed at birth, without reference to any preceding and prerequisite conditions. But on the contrary, it has been shown, that it is never conferred except upon two unchangable conditions. And that these conditions are, first, the possession of complete personal perfection, moral, mental and physical; and, second, admission to the tree of life.—See Gen. 3:22 and Rev. 22: 2, 3. It has been shown that moral perfection is to be attained in this life, by meeting the tests that God places upon our characters, and that mental and physical perfection will be conferred at the resurrection of the dead, and at the translation of the living saints; and that admission to the tree of life will soon follow these events. In harmony with the foregoing, and in confirmation thereof, it has been shown that the wicked are not, and never will be, immortal. They are to utterly perish and disappear. It has been proven from the Bible, that the wicked are to be consumed and forever vanish in the smoke of their torment. See Matt 3:12, Mark 9:44, where an undying worm—probably something like the horrible trichinae of of our day—infests their bodies until they are consumed. Further, see Jude 7, 2 Pet. 2:6, Rev. 14:11, Rev. 20:8, 9. Mal. 3:1, and a vast number of other passages.

Thus it has been made clear that the Bible, as well as common sense, and the very nature of things, teaches that imperfection and immortality do not go together. It is insisted that Paul means this, when, in 1 Cor. 15:50, he says, that "corruption doth not inherit incorruption;" or, in other words, the dying does not inherit the undying; the mortal does not inherit the immortal; And, if a mortal body could not inherit an undying, or immortal body, how much more is it evident that it could not inherit an immortal mind? It has, therefore, been held with Ezekiel, that "the soul that sinneth it shall die;" but on the other hand, "they that do his commandments may enter in through the gates into the city, have right to the Tree of Life. eat its precious fruit.

"Triumph in immoratal powers,
And clap their wings of fire."

But the Christian world reject this great truth. And having cast aside the teachings of the word of God in the matter, are about to call in Satan, and fallen angels, to give them a living demonstration that the original lie, told to Eve, is now the truth; for the soul is naturally immortal, and "ye shall not die." When this state of things is reached, as it soon will be, we shall have Babylon become the "habitation of devils" and "a hold of every foul spirit," and of those who hold communion with those "spirits," such as mediums, and all the officiary, and devotees of Spiritualism. We now charge upon the Christian world, that they shut their eyes to the light in reference to

THE STATE OF THE DEAD.

In harmony with the foregoing principle that man is not immortal in this life, it has been shown, that when he dies. every active principle of his being sinks into a state of suspense, or inaction, and that for this reason, death is called a sleep in the word of God. See 1 Cor. 15, and the many other places where the dead are spoken of as being asleep.

In connection with this fact it has been proven, that the dead get their reward at the last judgment, and not at death, in accordance with what our Savior said of those who invite the poor to their feasts, viz.: that "they should be recompensed at the resurrection of the just;" and in harmony with what Peter said, to the effect that, the "Lord reserves the unjust to the day of judgment to be punished." It has been, therefore, insisted, that the penitent thief on the cross would get his recompense for recognizing and believing in his dying Lord, at the resurrrection of the just, and not on the day it was promised to him. It has also been insisted, that Lazarus would also get his reward at the same resurrection of the just, when angels would escort him into the kingdom of God, to sit down with Abraham. It has been shown also, that the "rich man," spoken of in connection with Lazarus, would be reserved to the day of judgment to be punished; when, with all the wicked. he would be tormented in the flames. Thus it has been shown. that the dead are in a state of inaction, but that they will be resuscitated at the resurrection of the last day, at which time they will receive their reward. But the Christian world reject this plain truth, and are about to throw themselves into the arms of Spiritualism, that from it, they may get the proof, not to be found in the Bible, that the "dead are alive." We now proceed to charge the Christian world with rejecting light in regard to the

FUTURE STATE AND HEAVEN.

It has been abundantly shown. that heaven is a "place;" that it is a "country;" and that it contains a "city, which hath foundations whose builder and maker is God." See John 14: 1-3, Heb. 11: 14:16, and Rev. 21. It has been therefore, insisted, that heaven must be a planet, or world, similar to our own; without, however, the sins of men, or the curse of God. It has been shown that nothing less than such a heaven would be a suitable abode for unfallen angels, and for that great multitude of "redeemed men, of every nation, and kindred and tongue," which John saw standing before the throne, "clothed with white robes and palms in their hands;"

> "From every land redeemed to God;
> Arrayed in garments washed in blood."

The best of all is, it has been proven that the earth itself is to be renewed by the hand of God, and the blissful scenes there to be witnessed are similar to those above described as existing in heaven. In fact it has been shown. that the "city of our God," now located in heaven, with its glories, is to be transferred to the earth. See Isaiah 66:22, 2 Pet. 3:13, and Rev. 21 and 22.

But the Christian world reject these great facts and truths in regard to heaven and the future state. They insist that heaven is an "immaterial" abode of immaterial spirits, and they call it the "Spirit Land." We here suggest, that as these immaterial spirits are not quite satisfactory, and Satan is invited to come around and "materialize" them, to render them a little more tangible, why would it not be the proper thing to have Satan try his hand on the immaterial spirit land, and render it at least, slightly obvious, by materializing it ! ! How do the leaders of the Christian world avoid these great truths, in regard to immortality, the condition of the dead, and the future state? Do they answer the arguments by which they are proved? They do not, so far as we have ever heard, or read. It is so much easier, and it answers just as well, and may be a little better, the way matters are to cry, Materialism! Soul Sleeping!! and so on. There are soul sleepers. Yes, two kinds of them! One kind fall asleep when they die, and the other kind while they are yet alive. The first kind "sleep in Jesus," and the second, sleep in sin. If we had to make our choice between falling asleep at death, to rest in the keeping of God till the resurrection, and falling asleep while alive; to slumber on in false security, while the scheme of redemption closes up, and then wake to find that the devil had narcotized us to our destruction, we should choose the former, and congratulate ourselves that we were not in the same wagon with the other kind of soul sleepers. But further, the Christian world reject light in regard to

THE LAW OF GOD.

This law has been shown to be embraced in the ten commandments. In regard to these commandments it has been shown, that they embrace every thing that is right and exclude everything that is wrong, and, that, therefore, the world is founded upon them. It has been shown that all the duties and rights of men are included in them. It has been shown that the time allotted to men, by their Maker, is by that law, given to them in periods of seven days; and, that, during the first six them of them, they should "labor and do their work." Or, in other words, that God requires industry and activity at the hands of his creatures. On this commandment, then, rest all the right and honorable callings and employments of men. It is shown to be in perfect harmony with this part of the divine law, and necessarily growing out of it, that those who do "labor and do all their work" should have the right to appropriate the product, or proceeds of their labor; and that here the right of private, or individual, property, comes in. It is further shown that this law positively recognizes the right of private property when it says, "Thou shalt not steal;" and still more clearly when it says, "Thou shalt not covet anything that is thy neighbors." It is further shown, that this law recognizes the right of private property in land, when it says, "Thou shalt not covet thy neighbor's house." The house is a fixed abode. And it necessarily carries with it the right to the land on which it stands, and to as much adjacent territory as is necessary for the maintenance of the family, the servants, and all the animals connected with it.

It is further proven, that this law recognizes the family: for it requires children to honor and obey their parents, while it requires all the world to honor the tie of marriage between husband and wife. The right of life and reputation is also recognized in this code.

It is shown that out of industry, property, the family and the right of life and reputation spring all the original rights and duties of men towards each other. It is seen that all these rights are by this code carefully guarded against infraction, by those commandments which forbid killing, stealing, lying, coveting, or adultery, and disobedience to parents. And here, it is insisted, lies the right of men to form governments, to protect all the above rights; and to create any political duties necessary for that purpose.

But further, it is shown that religion is founded on this law. For it recognizes one God, who alone is described as the creator, and governor, of the world, and of the universe. The worship of this God is shown to be required by that part of this law which sets apart the last of the seven days as a day to be "kept holy,"—that is, this day is to be devoted to divine worship, and such other duties as are allied with it. The infraction of this part of the divine law is guarded by forbidding the worship of any and all other objects, and all irreverence to the true God.

Thus it is seen, that, in the ten commandments, we have a law that embraces and enjoins upon men all the original principles of right among men, and of duty to God. That it binds men together by great and strong bands; and, by bands equally great and strong, binds them to their God. And leaves them thus, under the providence of God, to work out their destiny, as part of the universe, which God has made, and of which he is the rightful head.

It has been further proven that the plan and system of life laid down in the ten commandments is absolutely perfect. It is impossible for the mind to pronounce that plan and system of life to be wrong in a single particular. It is therefore insisted that these commandments will never be changed, or done away, either wholly or in part. This is why the Savior said, "till heaven and earth pass, one jot, or one tittle, shall, in no wise, pass from the law." It is also shown that the Sabbath lies at the very foundation of this law, since it points to the creation of heaven and earth as its author, and as the sovereign to whom it holds the world answerable.

The Christian world reject this part of the divine Law; although it has been shown, that the seven days of the fourth commandment constitute the week as existing among all nations originally, and as still existing among the enlightened races of men; and in the face of the everywhere acknowledged fact, that Saturday is the seventh day of that week. It has been shown that Christ, and every apostle and prophet, and every inspired writer that ever lived, kept Saturday and no other day. It has been shown that the New Testament recognizes this day, and no other. Yet, in the face of all this, and much more, the Christian world refuse to submit to the plain requirements of the fourth commandment. And, by this refusal, set themselves against the authority of the divine law. For inspiration has said, "Whosoever shall break the law at one point is guilty of all."—See Jas. 2:10. That is to say, to break down the law at one point prepares the way to overthrow it at every point. If, after the Christian world have refused obedience to one of the commandments, the rest of the world take the hint, follow their example, and refuse obedience to the others, and an age of lawlessness and crime is brought in, who will be responsible? Is it not the Christian world who have reopened the flood gates to sin? And if the foundations of Society and the world are washed out by the rushing tide, will not the Christian world have the opportunity to reflect, that breaking down the authority of the law of God over the consciences of men is not a very good way to convert the world and bring in the millennium? But we further charge, that the leaders of the Christian world reject light in regard to

SUNDAY.

It has been shown that Sunday originated among the ancient heathen, and that, from this source, the Romish Church obtained it, and that it came from the last named source into the Protestant world. It has been shown that the circumstances, in every case where the first day of the week is mentioned. in the New Testament, prove that it is a working day. Moreover, and further, it has been well proven, that Sunday is the mark of the Beast, mentioned in Rev. 13 and 14.

But the leaders of the Christian world. in the face of all the foregoing clearly proven facts in regard to Sunday, still insist that they must keep Sunday in honor of our Savior's resurrection; although they know, that there is no weekly cycle whatever connected with his resurrection. He rose on the third day from the date of his death; and if a day is observed in honor of his resurrection it should be every third day; or one day in the year, at the expiration of every yearly cycle. Is it not evident that this way of honoring Christ will ultimately land our Protestant churches alongside of the Romish Church. whose apostasy crystalized around Sunday, and also alongside of the pagan world. whose apostasy also crystalized around Sunday? And is not the Protestant world fast undergoing the same process? Sunday is a denial of the authority of the Creator, because it is a denial of the fourth commandment, upon which the recognition of his authority has been shown to rest. This is why rebellion against God can found itself upon Sunday. With the foregoing. we

CLOSE THE LIST

of subjects. in regard to which we charge the Christian world with having rejected light, full and clear. from the word cf God. Did ever so much light fall upon one generation of men? Surely not, unless it was upon the Jewish nation in the days of Christ and his apostles. Is it any wonder that the churches of our day are fallen? How could it be otherwise? Is it not to be expected that their fall will be, not only simultaneous, but also commensurate with the light they have rejected? The rejection of great light brings great apostasy. And what is Apostasy?

Apostasy is falling from the favor of God, and being rejected by him. That this is what constitutes apostasy needs but little proof. Every person who cares for his Bible knows that this is true. Paul shows in the first chapter of Romans that God "gave the pagans up" because they did not "like to retain him in their knowledge." There were some things about God that they didn't want to know. so they shut their eyes and became "wilfully ignorant." And God gave them up. The Jewish nation was rejected because they rejected the light shed over them in the days of Christ. The papal power "fell away" from the truths of God's word. and then God rejected it. And we have just seen. that the fall of Protestantism is connected with the rejection of light. We now proceed to notice some of the results and consequences of apostasy. And we shall prove that one cf the first of these is

DELUSION.

When the Pagan world fell. God gave them over, and they soon came to believe that their gods had a real connection with the control of the world, and could render them assistance if they chose to. The Jews were "blinded" by their rejection of the Messiah, and to this day really believe that Christ was not the Messiah. The papal power believe that they are just about what they claim to be, viz.: the one only true church upon earth. And the Protestant world are about te experience a similar, or even greater delusion. The Christian world are about to fall under the delusion of believing that Satan is Christ. This seems to be foretold in 2 Thess. 2: 9—12, where it is shown, that just before the coming of the Lord, Satan will be working "with all power, and signs, and lying wonders, and, at the same time, there will be a class who will not receive the truth, and God will give them up to strong delusion to believe a lie. We shall probably soon see the Christian world accept Spiritualism as a genuine work of God, in which Satan will act in the role of Christ. But further, we now mention a second consequence of apostasy, in the development of

IMMORALITY.

Take the apostasy of the Pagan world as described in the first chapter of Romans, and see how, after God had given them up, they became "filled with all unrighteousness, fornication, wickedness, covetousness, maliciousness; full of envy, murder, debate, deceit, malignity; whisperers, back-biters, haters of God, despiteful, proud boasters, inventors of evil things, disobedient to parents without understanding, covenant breakers, without natural affection, implacable, unmerciful." A state of things similar to the above existed in the church of Rome, in the sins and crimes of the dark ages. And, according to the Bishop quoted in another part of this tract, many of these sins are common in the churches of our day. A third consequence of apostasy we understand to be a

POLITICAL RELIGION.

That is to say, a religion that seeks for the favor or support of the State. The pagans resorted to the authority of law to support their systems of idolatry. The Romish church, in her fall, allied herself with the civil power, in order to hold her ground. The Protestant world are now reaching out their hands and calling upon the civil power to come to their aid; and it is only a matter of time when her call will be heeded, and then, as politics and politicians, with all their "claquers and hangers on," come into the churches we shall have the age of Constantine repeated, and Babylon will become "a cage of every unclean and hateful bird." And this State of things will prepare the way for the fourth consequence of apostasy, which is

PERSECUTION.

God always has somebody ready to expose the situation when things come to such a crisis, and legal persecution is the result. Protestantism is about to follow in the wake of Rome, and repeat her efforts to domineer the consciences of men and silence every voice that is raised against its sins. The efforts being made by Protestants to gain a firmer footing on the basis of the civil power, can be understood as meaning nothing but that they design to enforce their religion upon all. Why are they so anxious for a closer union with the civil authority, if this is not their object? Thus we see many of the fruits of apostasy in our churches, while the very last and worst consequences of that state are looming into sight before our eyes. What effect must such a state of things have upon those who really fear God and honor his word, but are in fellowship with those churches? They will be obliged, by the necessities of the situation, to

COME OUT OF THEM.

Abraham had to separate from the pagans of his country, and kindred, and father's house. The followers of Christ, among the Jews, had to separate from their apostate brethren and be organized into a new body. The people of God had to separate from Rome in her apostasy, and retire into the wilderness, or mountains of Europe. And can the children of God, in the churches of our day. longer remain in their communion, without endangering themselves? They surely cannot witness the state of things and hold their peace. If they do, they will become partakers of their sins, and of their plagues. But, if they speak out, they will not be allowed to remain in the communion of those Churches. And what object could there be in remaining in their communion? There is no ground to hope that they can be reformed and restored. The history of the world does not furnish an instance of the reformation and restoration to God of a church, or nation, which had fallen from him. by the rejection of light sent them in his providence, unless it was the restoration of the Jews from their Babylonish captivity. There seems to be but two courses open before the children of God now in the churches of the land. And these are, to remain in them and perish; or leave them. "Come out of her my people." We have now arrived at the conclusion of this matter, and to that stage of our subject where the

SEVEN LAST PLAGUES

demand our attention. The judgments of God always follow apostasy. Upon the heathen world they have fallen thick and fast, in famines. pestilences, earthquakes, and desolating war. Upon the Jews. those judgments lit, like bolts of wrath, in the destruction of their city and nation, and their dispersion and suffering among all the nations. The papal world was scourged for ages, by the Mohammedan power, as well as by earthquakes, pestilences and wars. But the judgments to fall upon the Protestant world are not of a national or political. character. They are literal. For it will be seen by reading the account of them in Rev. 16, and also in Rev. 18, that they can hardly be understood on any other theory. The destruction of Babylon is literal, also, as will be seen by carefully reading the account of it. Under these plagues the apostate Christian world is to sink like a great mill-stone cast into the sea—to rise no more. And. with her, sink also to rise no more, apostate Rome, apostate Paganism. all together making an apostate world. "And the seventh angel poured out his vial into the air; and there came a great voice out of the temple of heaven. from the throne, saying,

IT IS DONE."

SPECIAL POINTS.

In the foregoing pages we have enumerated only the leading truths now rejected by the Christian world. But along, and connected, with these, are others, of scarcely less importance; among which we might mention;—the doctrine of the last priestly ministrations of Jesus Christ prior to his second coming —the doctrine of the United States in the light of prophecy—the doctrine of the three messages of Rev. 14—the doctrine that a new people must appear at this day to give those messages—and so on. In addition to all the truths that are rejected, it must be remembered, that, in rejecting a truth or doctrine of the Bible. not only is that truth or doctrine set aside. but every passage of Scripture which goes to prove that truth or doctrine is also set aside. For. denying a truth is simply denying the evidence on which that truth rests. If all the verses, and chapters and pages of the Bible. which go to prove the truths we have charged the Christian world with rejecting, were collected together, it would be seen that they comprise a large portion of that book.

It would be safe to say that such a collection would embrace at least one-half of the entire word of God. We believe it would embrace even more. Yet, the leaders of the churches set it aside, and deny the only logical and safe conclusions that can be drawn from it. What is this but rejecting that word? And, when men reject the word of God, do they not reject God himself? When men reject the plain and obvious teachings of Jesus Christ, do they not reject Jesus Christ himself? When men reject what was inspired by the Holy Spirit, do they not reject the Holy Spirit itself?

GRADUAL PROCESS.

The foregoing truths were not rejected simultaneously. They were not all laid before the churches and rejected at the same time. One after another they were developed, from the study of the sacred word, and rejected as fast as they were placed before the world. The doctrine of the second coming of Christ· was the first special truth laid before the Christian world of this generation. Then light came in regard to the nature of man, his condition in death, the end of the wicked, and in reference also to the character of the future world itself. Light, full and clear, broke out next in reference to the divine law; showing its unity, and its unchangeable, imperishable and indestructible nature; revealing Saturday as the true, and Sunday as a spurious Sabbath. This was followed by light in regard to the United States as the two-horned beast of Rev. 13, and Sunday as the "mark of the beast." This work has gone on--line upon line has been given--truth has been added to truth--until the broken and shattered system of the Christian religion is at last repaired and restored. The work begun by Wyckliffe, Huss, Luther, and others, and carried forward by a great host of our noble ancestry, is completed, and those who prize "the truth, the whole truth, and nothing but the truth," may now be gratified.

GREAT ERRORS.

Just as the foregoing truths have been laid before the Christian world and rejected by it, the same Christian world have taken up some error to which it adheres in place of the rejected truth. The second coming of Christ and destruction of the world are rejected, and in their place the conversion of the world and the millennium are taught. Instead of the doctrine of immortality through Christ at his coming, the natural and inherent immortality of the soul is taught. The law of God is rejected and an appeal is made to human law to come in and sway the consciences of men. We might specify many such errors, but it is not necessary. The three we have named--the millennium—human law—and natural immortality--constitute the foundations of a great system of error. A realm of a thousand years in this world human law to coerce the conscience in that realm and natural immortality, with which to soar away to heaven, without waiting for Christ to come after his people these are the main, stones in the foundation of that great temple of error, unto which it is expected soon to gather the whole world.

FINAL APOSTASY.

Another special point to which we invite attention is that the rejection of the foregoing truths not only brings apostasy, but it brings final and incurable apostasy. The heathen world had rejected no greater light when God left them and gave them up. The Jews had not refused more truth when they were cast off. The papal power had shown no greater hatred of divine truth when she was cast off and treated as anti-Christ. Besides this, the truths laid before the Christian world in our day, by special messages, are the last truths God has to offer. The messages of Rev. 14 are the last that the inhabitants of earth are to hear. And the truths with which those messages are burdened are the very truths which the churches of our day have rejected. Hence the apostasy of those churches is final and irremediable.

A DIRE NECESSITY.

No logic is necessary to prove—it is self-evident—that, when churches have reached such a degree of apostasy and rebellion against the word of God it is wrong to remain in communion with them. If it be true—and have we not shown that it is?—that our churches have rejected the last messages ever to be sent to them—if it be true that God has no more means avaible to reform them, what can men hope to accomplish? They can accomplish nothing. Every effort made only reveals anew the fact, that these churches are fully set against the plain teachings of the Bible. All, then, that persons who do not share this rebellion can do is—like the Israelites in Egypt—to pack up and leave; escape their sins and prepare to escape their judgments. Noah separated from the antediluvians, in order to escape their doom. Lot left the cities of the plain for the same reason. The followers of Christ had to make their flight from Jerusalem and Judea to avoid the destruction visited upon them. The time has now come when those who would escape the seven, last plagues, must forever separate from the fallen churches of the Christian world.

THE LAST CONFLICT.

Nothing is more sure than, that the proclamation of the apostasy of the christian world, and the consequent separation of God's true children from the churches, will bring on a collision between those churches and the people who make this proclamation. The churches will employ all their resources to suppress the proclamation or prevent it from reaching their people. And, when other means fail, it is more than likely, that these churches will unite in an appeal to the law. In that case, we shall have a revival of legalized persecution, which never stops short of inflicting death. When this stage is reached, the Christian world will have "filled the cup of her iniquities," and her career will be suddenly arrested by the second advent of our Lord Jesus Christ.

> "The Lord will come, but not the same
> As once, a lowly form he came—
> A weary man, and full of woes—
> A silent lamb before his foes.

> "The Lord will come—a dreadful form;
> With wreath of flame and robe of storm;
> On cherub wings and wings of wind—
> Anointed judge of human kind."

Thus will end the long controversy between Christ and Satan—and between the church of Jesus Christ and the apostate peoples of earth. Of Zion it may then be said—her conflicts are over—"her warfare is accomplished."

> "Triumphant Zion, lift thy head
> From dust, from darkness and the dead.
> Though humbled long, awake at length,
> And gird thee with thy Savior's strength.

> "No more shall foes unclean invade,
> Or fill thy hallowed walls with dread.
> No more shall hell's insulting host
> Their vict'ry, and thy sorrows, boast."

PART SECOND.

THE LOUD CRY.

We design now to show, that the foregoing pages contain the true basis of the Loud Cry. We shall also point out some erroneous views that are prevalent, to a greater or less extent, on this subject; and show how the loud cry is to be initiated; and what consequences will follow.

REVELATION 18.

We undertake to prove first, that the loud cry is based on the eighteenth chapter of Revelation. For proof we refer to chapter 38, vol. 4, Great Controversy. That chapter is entitled, "The Loud Cry;" and begins as follows:

"I saw another angel come down from heaven, having great power, and the earth was lightened with his glory. And he cried mightily, with a strong voice, saying, 'Babylon the great is fallen, is fallen; and is become the habitation of devils, and the hold of every foul spirit, and a cage of every unclean and hateful bird.'" "And I heard another voice from heaven saying, 'come out of her my people, that ye be not partakers of her sins, and that ye receive not of her plagues.'"

These are the first few verses of Rev. 18. And their being given, as they are, at the head of the chapter on the loud cry, shows that they constitute the foundation of that work. Read the entire chapter on the loud cry, in vol. 4, and there will be no doubt left in the mind of an Adventist that the loud cry is based on Rev. 18.

PARTICULAR POSITIONS.

Having just shown, in a general way, that Rev. 18 is the basis of the loud cry, we shall now undertake to prove, that the special positions taken in our treatise on the fall of Babylon, correspond with the positions to be taken in the loud cry. Again we quote from vol. 4:

"In this scripture, [Rev. 18], the announcement of the fall Babylon, as made by the second angel, is repeated, with the additional mention of the corruptions which have been entering the churches since 1844. A terrible condition of the religious world is here described. With every rejection of truth, the minds of the people have become darker, their hearts more stubborn, until they are intrenched in an infidel hardihood. In defiance of the warnings God has given, they continue to trample upon one of the precepts of the decalogue, and they persecute those who hold it sacred. Christ is set at naught, in the contempt placed upon his word and his people.—Page 421. On page 422 is the following language :

"Of Babylon at this time it is declared, 'her sins have reached unto heaven and God hath remembered her iniquities. She has filled up the measure of her guilt, and destruction is about to fall upon her.' But God still has a people in Babylon; and before the visitation of his judgments, these faithful ones must be called out, that they partake not of her sins, and receive not of her plagues. Hence the movement symbolized by the angel coming down from heaven, lightening the earth with his glory, and crying mightily with a strong voice, announcing the sins of Babylon. In connection with his message the call is heard, 'Come out of her my people.'" On page 424 is this language:

"The sins of Babylon will be laid open. The fearful results of a union of church and state, the inroads of spiritualism, the stealthy but rapid progress of the papal power—all will be unmasked. By these solemn warnings the people will be stirred. Thousands upon thousands have never listened to words like these. In amazement they hear the testimony that Babylon is the church, fallen because of her errors and sins, and because of her rejection of the truth sent to her from heaven."

The above quotations are sufficient for our purpose. We call attention to some statements contained in them. In several places the "rejection of truth" is referred to as one of the sins charged upon Babylon. For instance, on page 421 is this language : "With every rejection of truth the minds of the people have become darker." On page 424 we find this: "In amazement they hear the testimony, that Babylon is the church, fallen because of her errors and sins, and because of her rejection of the truth sent to her from heaven."

In the foregoing treatise on the fall of Babylon, we have taken the position, that her fall was caused by her rejection of truth. And we enumerated the leading truths which the Christian world reject. The rejection of these great truths lies at the very foundation of her fall. And her other sins, though many and great, are but the natural and logical consequences of the rejection of truth by her. If she had received the truths she has rejected, instead of falling lower and lower, she would have been rising in excellence. By rejecting so many great truths from the word of God, she has pulled down the barriers God had erected against sin and error, and thus opened the flood gates to every evil. So that it is now true, that Babylon is not only fallen, but is fast becoming the habitation of devils, the hold of every foul spirit, and a cage of every unclean and hateful bird. A process which will continue until she has filled up the cup of her iniquities, and God's judgments shall lay her low.

Notice some more statements in the quotations taken from vol. 4. On page 422 is this language:—Of Babylon at this time it is declared, her sins have reached unto heaven, and God hath remembered her iniquities. She has filled up the measure of her quilt, and destruction is about to fall upon her. This is in harmony with that part of our treatise where we show, that, in consequence of rejecting the last great messages and the truths which they offer, the rebellion of the Christian world against God has reached its climax, and her fall is, in consequence, final and eternal. That part of the sins of Babylon, which consist in the rejection of truth may already be said to have reached unto heaven. She has rejected all there is to reject; and she has filled up this part of the cup of her iniquities. Yet some of her secondary sins, or those that come in as consequences of rejecting truth, may not yet be fully developed. This part of the cup of her iniquities may not yet be quite full.

Another point we notice in the quotations from vol. 4 is, that under the loud cry, God's people will be called out of Babylon. On page 422 is this language:—"But God still has a people in Babylon; and before the visitation of his judgments, these faithful ones must be called out. In our treatise we have shown, that the fall of the churches, being final, no further effort to reform them will be made, and, therefore, God's people should be hurried out of them, as they are about to be destroyed by the last plagues.

The foregoing points of comparison are sufficient to show an exact harmony between our exposition of the eighteenth chapter of Revelation and what the fourth volume of the Great Controversy says on the subject of the "Loud Cry."

NECESSARY TO LOUD CRY.

We now venture the proposition, that the foregoing positions, drawn from

Rev. 18, are necessary to the loud c'' , and that, without them, there can be no loud cry. On page 422, vol. 4, aft ' brief sketch of the warnings to be drawn from Rev. 18, is this language:—'' ',/.:hese warnings join the third angel's message, it swells to a loud cry.'' Then these warnings must be joined with our present work in order to bring a¹-out the loud cry. And there can be no loud cry until they are so joined. The loud cry cannot be brought on in any other way.

ACTION OF THE GENERAL CONFERENCE.

The proposition, that the general conference is the highest ecclesiastical authority among Adventists needs no proof. It is also an admitted fact, that no new points of faith, or practice, can be brought in and adopted, but by the action of that body. Now, as there are new and special points in the eighteenth chapter of Revelation, and as those points have not yet been united with the third angel's message, it follows, that here is work for the general conference. That body will have to investigate these matters, and decide as to what constitutes the special warnings of Rev. 18. When this inquiry has been made in the providence of God, and decided in harmony with whatever may be the truth in the premises, we shall have the foundation laid for the loud cry; and will have the right to expect that feature of the third angel's message to begin. But until such investigation and decision of the general conference is had, we need not expect to see the loud cry set in. But while the action of the general conference is necessary, as shown above, the light with reference to Rev. 18, and the loud cry, will not originate with that body. In the first instance it will be brought forward by

NON-OFFICIAL PERSONS.

This fact is stated on page 424 of vol. 4. The language is as follows:—"As the time comes for the loud cry to be given, the Lord will work through humble instruments, leading the minds of those who consecrate themselves to his service. The laborers will be qualified by the unction of his Spirit, rather than by the training of literary institutions." This quotation shows, that those to whom this light is first committed are in humble stations, that they do not receive this light from literary institutions, nor from any other persons whatever, but from the Spirit of God, which leads their minds into it. It proves, also, that before the loud cry actually begins, God will be working through these persons to prepare the way for the loud cry. When this preliminary work has been done, and the general conference has also taken suitable action in the matter, then it may be said, that the angel of Rev. 18 has united with the third angel. We may then hope to witness the most important and thrilling

CONSEQUENCES.

Some of these consequences are described in vol. 4, pp. 429, 430. It is there declared, that:—"The angel who unites in the proclamation of the third message is to lighten the whole earth with his glory." A work of world-wide extent, and unwonted power, is here brought to view. The Advent movement of 1840-44 was a glorious manifestation of the power of God. The first message was carried to every missionary station in the world, and in this country there was the greatest religious interest which has been witnessed in any land since the reformation of the sixteenth century. But these are to be far exceeded by the mighty movement under the loud cry of the third message. The work will be similar to that of the day of pentecost." "By thousands of voices, all o \r t e earth, the message will be given." "The message will be carried, as was the midnight cry of 1844, not so much by arguments, as by the deep con-

viction of the Spirit of God. The ar   nents have been presented. The seed
has been sown, and now it will sprin   ) and bear fruit. The publications
distributed by missionary workers ha   xerted their influence. Yet many,
whose minds have been impressed, have been prevented from fully compre-
hending the truth, or from yielding obed' nce. Now the rays of light pene-
trate everywhere. The truth is seen in its clearness, and the honest children of
God sever the bands which held them.''

As another consequence of the loud cry, and the power attending it, the
''conflict'' is brought on. In vol. 4, p. 425, is this language:—''The power attending the message only maddens those who oppose it. The clergy put forth
almost snperhuman efforts to shut away the light, lest it should shine upon
their flock. By every means at their command they endeavor to suppress the
discussion of these vital questions. The church appeals to the strong arm of
civil power; and, in this work, papists are solicited to come to the help of Protestants. The movement for Sunday enforcement becomes more bold and decided.
The law is invoked against commandment keepers.'' Thus it is made clear.
that the conflict and persecution are the result of the loud cry, and not, that the
loud cry is the result of persecution.

TWO ERRORS.

In view of all that precedes, we can easily detect any errors that may have
obtained a recognition among us in regard to the loud cry. There are two errors somewhat current on this subject. One is—that the loud cry is, or may
now be, in progress. in our extensive missionary operations, and the world-
wide circulation of our literature. In the light of a foregoing quotation from
vol. 4, p. 43). we can safely say. that these things precede. and prepare the
way for. the loud cry; but they are not the loud cry The second error we
notice is this —that we are not to expect any special person, or persons, to arise
among us with the light in reference to the loud cry; or. that special measures
will have to be taken to bring it about. This last idea. we are informed, is being adopted by some of the leading men. But it is evidently an error. and one
that is of recent origin.

CONCLUSION.

As a conclusion to this publication, and as a confirmation of the things
contained in it. and as its chief attraction. we quote. entire. the chapter on the
loud cry in Early Writings. beginning on page 137. It reads as follows:

''I saw angels hurrying to and fro in heaven, descending to earth and
again ascending to heaven. preparing for the fulfillment of some important
event. Then I saw another mighty angel commissioned to descend to earth, to
unite his voice with the third angel. and give power and force to his message.
Great power and glory were imparted to the angel. and, as he descended, the
earth was lightened with his glory. The light which attended this angel
penetrated everywhere. as he cried mightily. with a strong voice. saying,
'Babylon. the great. is fallen. is fallen. and is become the habitation of devils.
and the hold of every foul spirit, and a cage of every unclean and hateful bird.'
The message of the fall of Babylon. as given by the second angel. is repeated.
with the additional mention of the corruptions which have been entering the
churches since 1844. The work of this angel comes in at the right
time to join in the last great work of the third angel's message, as it swells
to a loud cry. And the people of God are prepared to stand in the hour of
temptation which they are soon to meet. I saw great light resting upon them.
and they united to fearlessly proclaim the third angel's message.

Angels were sent to aid the mighty angel from heaven. And I heard voices which seemed to sound everywhere —'Come out of her, my people, that ye be not partakers of her sins, and that ye receive not of her plagues; for her sins have reached unto heaven, and God hath remembered her iniquities.'

The message seemed to be an addition to the third message, joining it, as the midnight cry joined the second angel's message of 1844. The glory of God rested upon the patient, waiting saints, and they fearlessly gave the last solemn warning, proclaiming the fall of Babylon. and calling upon God's people to come out of her, that they might escape her fearful doom. The light that was shed upon the waiting ones penetrated everywhere; and those in the churches who had not heard and rejected the three messages, obeyed the call and left the fallen churches. Many had come to years of accountability since the messages had been given, and the light shone upon them, and they were privileged to choose life or death. Some choose life, and took their stand with those who were looking for their Lord, and keeping all his commandments. The third message was to do its work. All were to be tested upon it, and the precious ones were to be called out of the religious bodies. A compelling power moved the honest, while the manifestation of the power of God brought a fear, and a restraint, upon their unbelieving relatives and friends; so that they dared not, neither had they the power to, hinder those who felt the work of the Spirit of God upon them. The last call was carried even to the poor slaves; and the pious among them poured forth their songs of rapturous joy, at the prospect of their happy deliverance. Their masters could not check them. Fear and restraint kept them silent. Mighty miracles were wrought, the sick were healed, and signs and wonders followed the believers. God was in the work, and every saint, fearless of consequences, followed the dictates of his own conscience, and united with those who were keeping all the commandments of God, and, with power, they sounded abroad the third message. I saw that this will close with power and strength far exceeding the midnight cry.

Servants of God, endowed with power from on high, with their faces lighted up and shining with holy consecration, went forth to proclaim the message from heaven. Souls that were scattered all through the religious bodies answered to the call, and the precious were hurried out of the doomed churches, as Lot was hurried out of Sodom before her destruction. God's people were strengthened by the excellent glory which rested upon them in rich abundance, and prepared them to endure the hour of temptation. I heard a multitude of voices saying —'here is the patience of the saints. Here are they that keep the commandments of God, and the faith of Jesus.' "

"Ye who rose to meet the Lord;
Ventured on his faithful word;
Faint not now, for your reward
Will be quickly given.
Faint not, always watch and pray.
Jesus will no more delay.
Even now 'tis dawn of day—
Day-star beams from heaven."

"Tones of thunder, through the sky—
Angel voices sounding high—
Echo still the mighty cry.
'Jesus quickly come.'"

"Even so, come. Lord Jesus. Come quickly."

PART THIRD.*

OUR DEFENSE.

By this, we mean, our defense against Butler, Jones, and the Kansas City church. The views expressed in the foregoing parts of this pamphlet, and our connection with them, have brought upon us the malediction of these parties.

CENSURED.

We were censured by the church in Kansas city. In order to give an idea as to how this censure came to be passed, we shall have to give a brief sketch of D. T. Shireman and his connection with our people. He became a professed Adventist in Iowa, years ago. In the days of Snook and Brinkerhoff he was strongly inclined to go with them, and did go so far as to sign a written statement intended to prove Mrs. White guilty of lying. Subsequently he went to Chicago. Then tried Topeka. Next, he appeared in Kansas City. Kansas City is a new and growing place. Many Adventists have gone there to get work, and this has caused quite a church to spring up. Mr. Shireman goes to every newly arrived Adventist, appears very pious, gets him into his confidence, and under his influence, and, in this way, builds himself up. He pretends to have labored there at a great financial sacrifice. But this is not true. He has been well paid. Considering the small amount, and poor quality, of his labor, he has been the best paid man that ever had any connection with our work.

Another special point with this man is, to break down and drive out of the church those whom he cannot control. Sr. Foster and her daughters moved to Kansas City. Mr. S. sought to buy their confidence and submission by pretended charity. When it became evident that he could not keep this intelligent and educated family under his control, he determined to destroy them. He circulated the most villainous lies through the church, in regard to Sr. Foster and her daughters, although they were also members of the church. The church forever silenced those lies, but failed to expel the slanderer. This family have been driven from the church, by Shireman's crimes.

On account of these matters, and in view of Shireman's ignorance, and lack of qualification, we opposed his election as elder of the church. For doing so, and for holding the views expressed in this pamphlet, on the "fall of Babylon," and the "loud cry," Jones got us censured. The censure was passed without any reply being made to what we had said, or any investigation as to its truth; though we demanded such an investigation. And we were silenced, by Jones, when we undertook to show that the censure should not be passed.

The investigation into the truth of the charges we made against Shireman, and which the church refused, we now demand, at the hands of the Mo. Conference. In regard to the church in Kansas City, we demand, that it be disbanded, its records burnt, and that a new church be organized, with Sr. Foster at its head. In regard to this man Shireman, we demand, that he be utterly separated from the people of God, and left to meet his reward in the billows of that "lake of fire" which he so much, and so justly dreads. For, that God who has no crimes to cover up by being "righteous overmuch," can endure him no longer.

---

*We had no thought of writing this part when the cover and title-pages were printed. For this reason the title to this part does not appear on them.

DISFELLOWSHIPPED.

We now proceed to show how Jones got the Kansas City church to disfellowship us. By the assistance of letters, written by G. I. Butler, a conspiracy was formed between S. M. Ford and his wife, Missouri Kester, and the judges of the Circuit Court, in Kansas City, to rob me of my child. They tore her from me, and placed her in an asylum for children who had no one to take care of them. At this place there were nearly a hundred children "of all sorts." There were two or three women there to look after them. My child had to sleep in the same bed with three others. Said she did not get enough to eat. Her hair was not combed during three days, and, on the next day, they were going to cut her hair off close to her head. She had no attention, and had to take care of herself. She had to go to bed at sunset, even though it was in the winter. But she said, "this was the best part about it;" for, then, she could cry all she wanted to, and she would lie there and cry all night. Her heart was broken with grief. When I would go to see her and start away, she would throw her arms about my neck, to keep me from going, while streams of tears ran down her anguished face. I would have to force myself away from her. I pray God to forgive me. After leaving her there three days, I took her away, "without leave or license;" and this is what Jones calls. "a crime against the laws of Mo." And this is the "unlawful and disorderly conduct" Jones got us disfellowshipped for.

Now, instead of this being a violation of the law of Mo., we will show that I would have violated the law of this state if I had not taken her away. Section 1273, p. 224, of the Revised Statutes of Mo., being the law now in force, says: If any man shall, without good cause, * abandon his child or children under the age of twelve years, * and shall fail. neglect or refuse to maintain and provide for such * child or children, he shall, upon conviction. be punished by imprisonment in the county jail not more than one year, or by a fine of not less than fifty, nor more than one thousand, dollars, or by both such fine and imprisonment."

According to this, it was my duty to take my child and properly care for her, unless the action of the above mentioned conspirators, in putting her there, was a "good cause" why I should "fail, neglect, or refuse" to provide for her.

We will now prove, that this was not only not a good cause why I should leave my child in such a place, but that it was a

PENITENTIARY OFFENSE

in Gill, Slover, and others, to take her from me and put her there. But before we bring forward the special Mo. law whose penalty they have incurred, we wish to place before the reader a brief view of the law, on the subject of "Fathers and their children." We will begin by quoting the greatest American writer upon the law, viz: Chancellor Kent. In Kent's Commentaries, vol. 2, p. 182, is this language:

"The wants and weaknesses of children render it necessary that some person maintain them, and the voice of nature has pointed out the parent as the most fit and proper person. The laws and customs of all nations have enforced this plain precept of universal law."

Again, in his Commentaries, vol. 2, p. 213, the same author says:

"The father (and on his death the mother) is generally entitled to the custody of the infant children, inasmuch as they are their natural protectors, for maintenance and education."

According to this great authority, the right of the parent to the custody of his children is founded in the law of nature, and sanctioned and upheld by the laws of all nations. We might fill a volume with quotations, to the same effect, from all the great writers on general law, and from the decisions of high courts in cases involving this principle. We will now prove that the law of Missouri is in perfect harmony with the above. Section 2560, page 432, of the Revised Statutes of Missouri, now in force, says :

"In all cases not otherwise provided for by law, the father; while living, and after his death. the mother, if living, shall be the natural guardian and curator of their children, and have the custody and care of their persons, education and estates."

So deeply is this principle imbedded in the law of nature and in the laws of the world, that high courts have held, that a father cannot divest himself of right, and any agreement he makes to this effect. even though made with his wife. is null and void. Kent's Commentaries, Vol. 2, pp. 213,214, note C, says :

"In the case of the People against Mercien, it was, after an elaborate discussion. * * * declared that the husband could not. by agreement with his wife. alienate to her his right to the custody of their children. and the agreement." made for this purpose, "was void."—See 3 Hill.

If he could not alienate this right to his wife, certainly he could to no one else. There is only one way in which a father's right to his children can pass from him. He may, by negligence, or cruelty. or inability, or crime, forfeit this right. Kent's Commentaries, Vol. 2, p. 213 note h, says:

"The courts award children to the father," unless he had abused the right to the custody of his child, or there be an apprehension of cruelty, or some exhibition of gross profligacy, or want of ability to provide for his children.' On the same page is the language of Chancellor Kent, himself, as follows :

The courts of justice may, * when the morals, or safety. or interests of the children strongly require it. withdraw the infants from the custody of the father or mother, and place the care and custody of them elsewhere."

These are the causes for which a father's child may be taken from him, and there is no law in heaven or earth—nor in Missouri—to take his child from him for any minor cause. Are these, or any of them. the reason why our child was torn from us? No. No such causes were assigned. But one of the judges had promised his fellow conspirators privately. that, if they would bring the case up, he would take our child from us. And they took her in violation of every law, both human and divine; and in violation of Section 1270, p. 223 of the Revised Statutes of Missouri. which says:

"Every person who shall. maliciously, forcibly or fraudulently, lead. take or carry away, or decoy or entice away, any child under the age of twelve years, with the intent to detain or conceal such child from its parent, guardian or other person having the lawful charge of such child, shall upon conviction, be punished by imprisonment in the penitentiary not exceeding five years. or in a county jail not exceeding six months, or by fine not less than five hundred dollars."

It is now clear, that those who robbed us of our child are criminals. and ought to be in the penitentiary. Yet Jones says. we are the one who is guilty of the "crime" of violating this section of the laws of Mo. !!! We pass this subject now and take up

JONES'. LETTER.

We do not mean his letter to the churches in regard to us, but a certain letter he wrote to us last summer, and which is now in our possession. There is only one point in it that we notice now. We wrote him, thinking we would try to adjust the difficulties we had with K. C. Church, if it could be done honorably. We were not aware, at the time we wrote him, that he had got the church to expel us for crime. In his reply to us he puts himself on record as follows:

"One year ago you was out of the church. You came to me and wanted a place in the church, and expressed yourself as willing to take the lowest place. I interceded for you and you was taken in." But this is not all. After accusing us of not keeping our promise, he says:

"Now it seems strange that you would turn and ask me to do the same thing over again, when you did not keep faith with me before."

His statements, so far as they relate to our doing any such things are utterly untrue. But in what light do they present Jones? It appears, that he looks upon membership in the church af if it were a matter of patronage for him to dispose of on such terms as he might see fit. And he claims that he actually agreed with us that we might become a member on condition that we would take the "lowest place." He says, that he actually got us into the church with this understanding. He says, that we did not keep our promise, and he "won't do so any more!" According to this Jones, we must be kept out of the church altogether, unless we will take and keep the "lowest place." In other words, we must crouch down in a corner, like an obedient dog, and not open our mouth, or stay out of the church ! ! This brings us to another point in the case of Jones. We can now see why he is so anxious to have Missouri Adventists shut us

OUT OF THEIR HOUSES.

Men, who are guilty of such things as he is, do not like to have any one "tell on" them. If they happen to be in office, and have a little authority, they are sure to call up the "gag law," and either silence the man who exposes them, or persuade, or order, people not to listen. This remark will apply to what was said and done, at the last Conference, in regard to us. We do not know what it was that was there said and done, neither do we care. That which is done against a man in his absence, and without even a pretense of investigating his grievances, is worthy only of contempt.

The above will do on the subject of Jones. What has he done? It is safe to say that he has successfully "exposed his ignorance," and his malice against us. He has shown also that he has not as much soul in him as a common brute has, or he would not have accused us of crime in taking our child. D(isgusting) T(hing) Jones! Mental and moral idiot ! ! He is now placed at Battle Creek by the hand of Providence, so that the whole denomination can have a good look at him, before he disappears forever. We demand that he be silenced from the ministry, entirely separated from the work of God, expelled from the church, and left to vanish in smoke, amid the ill-flavored fumes of the damned.

G. I. BUTLER.

In Testimony No. 25, there is a chapter under the title "Leadership." This chapter was an original testimony given to G. I. Butler. From it we quote what follows:

"You are too slow. You should cultivate opposite qualities. The cause of

God demands men who can see quickly, and act instantaneously, at the right time. and with power. If you want to measure every difficulty, and balance every perplexity you meet, you will do but little. You will have difficulties and obstacles to encounter at every turn, and you must with firm purpose,decide to conquer them, or they will conquer you. Sometimes various ways and purposes, different modes of operation in connection with the work of God. are about evenly balanced in the mind. But it is at this very point that the nicest discrimination is necessary. And, if anything is accomplished, it must be done at the golden moment. The slightest inclination in the balance should be seen and determine the matter at once. * It is more excusable to make a wrong decision sometimes than to be in a universal wavering position. hesitating, sometimes inclined in one direction, then in another. More perplexities, and wretched results, attend this hesitating and doubting than to sometimes move too hastily. My brother, you need to cultivate promptness. Away with your hesitating manner. You are slow, and neglect to seize the work and accomplish it. You must get out of this narrow manner of labor, for it is of the wrong order. When unbelief takes hold of your soul, your labor is of such a hesitating. halting. balancing kind, that you accomplish nothing yourself, and hinder others from doing. You have just enough interest to see difficulties and start doubts, but have not the interest, or courage, to overcome the difficulties. or dispel the doubts. At such times you need force of character. less stubbordness, and set willfulness. and you need to surrender to God. This slowness, this sluggishness of action. is one of the greatest defects in your character. and stands in the way of your usefulness. Your slowness of decision in connection with the cause of God is sometimes painful. It is not all necessary. Prompt and desisive action will accomplish great results. You are generally willing to work when you feel just like it: ready to do when you see clearly what is to be done. But you fail to be the benefit to the cause you might if you were prompt and decisive at the critical moment, and would overcome the hesitation and delay which have marked your character, and which have greatly retarded the work of God. This defect, unless overcome. will prove, in instances of great crises, disastrous to the cause. and fatal to your own soul."

In addition to the above, this man is now guilty of brutality, lying, slander, and other crimes. The crowd he belongs with, and the place where he will get his reward, are described in Rev. 22:15: "For without are dogs. and sorcerers and whoremongers, and murderers, and idolaters, and whosoever loveth and maketh a lie."

We demand that he be silenced from the ministry, separated wholly and forever. from the work of God. expelled from the church. and left to sink into hell, branded — liar — slanderer — tyrant—brute — sensualist — fool. Exit.— G(reat) I. B(e).

MRS. WHITE.

It will seem strange to see this name here. Are we going to denounce her also? No. But we are going to quote her. In her article in the Review of Sep. 4. 1888, was the following language:

"The most useful men in the world have not been the exalted, self-sufficient ones, who have been petted and praised by society; but those who have walked humbly with God. who have been unassuming in manner. and guileless in conversation. who have given all the glory to God. not taking any of it to themselves, are the ones who have exerted the most decided and healthful influence upon the church, * they exert their God-given ability to set things in order in the church, whether it makes them friends or foes. When straight, solemn testimony is needed in rebuking sin and iniquity, even though it be in those of high position. they will not hold their peace, but will heed the instruction of the God of truth, when he commands—'Cry aloud, spare not, lift up thy voice like a trumpet, and show my people their transgressions, and the house of Jacob thine sins.' They will stand as faithful watchmen on the walls of Zion, not to hide sin, not to flatter the wrong-doer, not to obtain the sympathy of their brethren, but to meet the approval of God. They will not suppress one syllable of truth that should be brought out, in reproof or warning, or in vindication of the righteousness of the oppressed, in order to gain the favor and influence of any one. In a crisis, they will not be found in a neutral position, but they will stand firmly on the side of righteousness and truth, even when it is difficult to take this position; and to maintain it, may imperil their prosperity, and deprive them of the friendship of those whom they love."

What are we to conclude from the above language? It is certainly an evident fact, that there are men in "high positions" among us who are guilty of "sin and iniquity." It is also certain that some one must and will expose these men's "sin's and iniquities;" and that this will bring on a "crisis." The very character of some of the "iniquities" of these men is plainly pointed out where certain ones are spoken of as "oppressed;" and a part of the nature of the "crisis" is brought to view where the "vindication" of these oppressed persons is spoken of. In plain English, then. the facts are these: Some of our high officers are guilty of "iniquity," and are also tyrants. and guilty of using their authority and official influence to "oppress" somebody, and the exposure of their sins, and the "vindication" of those who are "oppressed" will bring on a "crisis" in the church. This crisis must now be at hand, or the Spirit of God would not have prompted such language at this time. In this crisis true men will not remain

NEUTRAL.

The language above quoted says:—"They (true men) will not remain neutral, but they will stand firmly on the side of righteousness and truth, even though it will be difficult to take this position." In this crisis every one must take sides, and stand firmly by "righteousness and truth." But it will not be easy to do this, owing to the powerful influence men in high position wield. Where in the world is this impending "crisis," if not in Missouri? Here it is, and no mistake; and it is a crisis that will not "down at the bidding" of a "little brief authority." It is a crisis that will extend beyond Missouri, and it will eventuate in the "shaking" described in Early Writings. and in the loud cry. When it has been passed through, the aspect of things will be quite different. Till then, we gird ourselves for battle, in favor of a renovated church.

"I love thy kingdom, Lord—
The house of thine abode—
The church our blest Redeemer saved
With his own, precious blood.

"I love thy church, O God,
Her walls before thee stand—
Dear as the apple of thine eye,
And graven on thy hand.

"For her, my tears shall fall.
For her, my prayers ascend,
To her my cares and toils be given,
Till toils and cares shall end.

"Sure as thy truth shall last,
To Zion shall be given,
The brightest glories earth can yield,
And brighter bliss of heaven."

Part Fourth.

THE SHAKING.

Here is another addition to our pamphlet. We had no thought of writing it till Part Third was in the printer's hands. By the shaking, we mean, the special shaking described in Early Writings, p. 131, *et seq.* Before we can give a clear idea of this, we shall have to place before you a brief description of the condition of our denomination. We shall begin with the

MINISTRY.

"Our ministers are not doing their whole duty."—Testimony 31, p. 5. "Satan is constantly at work to break down the strongholds which debar him from free access to souls; and while our ministers are no more spiritually minded, while they do not connect closely with God, the enemy has great advantage, and the Lord holds the watchman accountable for his success." "My brethren, ministers and laymen, I have been shown that you must labor in a different manner from what you have been in the habit of working. Pride, envy, self-importance, and unsanctified independence, have marred your labors. When men permit themselves to be flattered by Satan, the Lord can do little for them, or through them."—T. 31. p. 12. "My younger brethren in the ministry, * * God has sent you to be a light to the world by your good works, as well as by your words and theories. But many of you may truly be represented by the foolish virgins, who took no oil in their lamps."—T. 31, p. 17.

"Much of the preaching of late begets a false security."—T. 31, p. 100. "The truth is shorn of its power when preached by men who are seeking to display their learning and ability. Such men display, also, that they know very little of experimental religion, and they are unsanctified in life, and are filled with vain conceit. They do not learn of Jesus. They cannot present to others a Savior with whom they are not acquainted."—T. 31, p. 155. "I looked to see the humility of soul that should ever sit as a fitting garment upon our ministers, but it was not upon them. I looked for the deep love for souls that the Master said they should possess, but they had it not. I listened for the earnest prayers offered with tears and anguish of soul because of the impenitent in their own houses and in the church, but heard them not. I listened for appeals made in the demonstration of the Spirit, but missed them. * A few earnest humble ones were seeking the Lord. At some of the camp meetings one or two ministers felt the burden. * But a large majority of the ministers had no more sense of the sacredness of their work than children." "There are many flippant talkers of Bible truth, whose souls are as barren of the Spirit of God as were the hills of Gilboa of dew and rain."—T. 31. p. 162.

"No matter who you are. or what you have been, you can be saved only in God's appointed way. You must fall helpless on the rock. Christ Jesus. You must feel your need of a physician, and the one only remedy for sin, the blood of Christ. This remedy can be secured only by repentance toward God, and faith toward our Lord Jesus Christ. Here the work is yet to be begun by many who profess to be Christians, and even to be ministers of Christ."—T. 31, pp. 214, 215. "Some who profess to be spokesmen for God are in their daily life denying their faith. They present to the people important truths, but who are impressed by these truths? Who are convicted of sin? The hearers know. that those who are preaching to-day, to-morrow will be the first to join in pleasure, mirth and frivolity. Their influence out of the pulpit soothes the consciences of the impenitent, and causes the ministry to be despised. They themselves are asleep upon the verge of the eternal world."—T. 31, p. 186.

"Presidents of Conferences should be men who can be fully trusted with God's work. * They, even more than other ministers, should set an example of holy living, and of unselfish devotion to the interests of God's cause, that those looking to them for an example may not be misled. But in some instances they are trying to serve both God and mammon. They are not self-denying. * When the cause of God is wounded they are not bruised in spirit. * In their hearts they doubt the testimonies of the Spirit of God. They know not the fervent love of Jesus. And they are not faithful shepherds of the flock over which they have been made overseers. Their record is not one they will rejoice to meet in the Day of God."—T. 32, pp. 135, 136.

"Many who preach the truth to others are themselves cherishing iniquity." —T. 31, p. 72. "I tell you, not a few ministers who stand before the people to explain the Scriptures are defiled. Their hearts are corrupt; their hands are unclean."—T. 31, p. 74.

An address written by Mrs. White, in 1886, but which G. I. Butler does not allow to be circulated among our people, speaks of "men and women of large experience, who have been considered patterns of piety, as 'unsanctified, unholy, impure in thought, debased in conduct.'" The same address says:— "Let our ministers and workers realize, that it is not increase l light that they need, so much as it is to live out the light they already have. Preaching the most solemn truths to the people to-day, and then falling into the most abominable practices to-morrow, will not answer." The same address has this:— "Because great light has been given—because men have, as did the princes of Israel, ascended to the mount, and been privileged to have communion with God, and been allowed to dwell in the light of his glory,—for these, thus favored, to think that they can afterward sin, and corrupt their ways before God, is a fatal deception. * These great manifestations by God should never lull to security, or carelessness. They should never give license to licentiousness, or cause the recipients to feel that God will not be critical with them, because they think he is dependent on their knowledge and ability to act a part in the great work." Again this address says: "Fornication is in our ranks: I know it, for it has been shown me to be extending and strengthening its pollutions. Cleanse the camp of this moral corruption, if it takes the highest men in the highest positions." The above will do on this topic. We shall now give some evidence as to the state of the

PEOPLE.

We are at a loss where to begin, since there is so much on this point. As on the preceding point, we can only give a small portion of the evidence. But we begin where we first open Testimony No. 31. "I have been shown that the spirit of the world is fast leavening the church. You are following the same path as did ancient Israel. There is the same falling away from your holy calling as God's peculiar people. You are having fellowship with the unfruitful works of darkness. Your concord with believers has provoked the Lord's displeasure. You know not the things that belong to your peace, and they are being fast hid from your eyes. Your neglect to follow the light will place you in a more unfavorable position than the Jews upon whom Christ pronounced a woe.

"I have been shown that unbelief in the Testimonies has been steadily increasing, as the people backslide from God. It is all through our ranks, all over the field. But few know what our churches are to experience. I saw that at present, we are under divine forbearance; but no one can say how long this will continue. No one knows how great the mercy that has been exercised toward us. But few are heartily devoted to God. There are only a few who like stars in a tempestuous night, shine here and there among the clouds.

"Our people are making very dangerous mistakes. We cannot praise and flatter any man without doing him a great wrong; those who do this will meet with serious disappointment. They trust too fully to finite man, and not enough to God, who never errs. The eager desire to urge men into public notice is an evidence of backsliding from God, and friendship with the world. It is the spirit which characterizes the present day. It shows that men have not the mind of Jesus. Spiritual blindness and poverty of soul have come upon them. Often persons of inferior minds look away from Jesus to a merely human standard, by which they are not made conscious of their own littleness, and hence have an undue estimate of their own capabilities and endowments. There is among us, as a people, an idolatry of human instrumentalities and mere human talent, and these even of a superficial character. * God's people have departed from their simplicity. They have not made God their strength, and they are weak and faint spiritually.—T. 31, pp. 70, 71. This quotation contains the principal features of the spiritual apostasy of our people. It is not necessary to add to it. Yet we will give a brief passage from Mrs. White's article in the Review of July 24, 1888. It reads—"Spiritual death has come upon the people that should be manifesting life and zeal, purity and consecration, by the most earnest devotion to the cause of truth. The facts concerning the real condition of the people of God speak more loudly than their profession, and make it evident that some power has cut the cable that anchored them to the eternal rock, and that they are drifting away to sea, without chart or compass." These facts in regard to our ministry and people, reveal to every true Adventist, a

SAD CONDITION

of things. We are about to be brought into a fearful conflict with the powers of darkness. If we should go into this conflict, in our present condition, what would be the result? Would not such ministers and leaders betray us, desert their colors, and leave the field in possession of the enemy? Would not such people follow them, and fly before the foe? We know they would. But we will prove it.

"The time is not far distant, when the test will come to every soul. The Mark of the Beast will be urged upon us. Those who have step by step yielded to worldly demands, and conformed to worldly customs, will not find it a hard matter to yield to the powers that be, rather than subject themselves to derision, insult, threatened imprisonment and death. * *' * Many a star that we have admired for its brilliancy will then go out in darkness. Chaff like a cloud will be borne away on the wind, from places where we see only floors of rich wheat.—T. 31, p. 77. Our ship is about to enter stormy and perilous seas. Would it be safe, in her present condition, to launch her out to confront the foam-crested billows of opposition she is about to meet? We think not. But we will prove it.

"Important interests in the cause of God cannot be wisely managed by those who have had so little real connection with God as some of our ministers have had. To entrust the work to such men, is like setting children to manage great vessels at sea. Those who are destitute of heavenly wisdom, destitute of living power with God, are not competent to steer the gospel ship amid icebergs and tempests. The church is passing through severe conflicts, but in the hour of her peril, many would trust her to hands that would surely wreck her. We need a pilot on board now; for we are nearing the harbor." God forbid that our ship should be wrecked on the very rocks that lie "along the heavenly coast."

WHAT SHALL BE DONE?

Are all our ministers and leaders corrupt and treacherous? Are all our people unreliable? No. Thank God, we have generals who never showed the "white feather," and who never will. Thank God, we have soldiers who will respond to the call of that bugle "that never calls retreat."

Thank God, we have pilots and mariners who fear not the stormiest seas. "There are a few who like the stars in a tempestuous night, shine here and there among the clouds."—T. 31, p. 72. "But there are only a few" such. "But few are heartily devoted to God." Same place.

When these few devoted ones wake up to a sense of the situation, and realize the state of things surrounding them, and the dangers before them, they will go to work to set things in order in the church, and this will surely bring on

A COLLISION

between them and the great mass of the denomination, both ministers and people. This collision will bring great trials upon the small company who bring it on. It is the "crisis" that is now at hand, and that Mrs. White spoke of in the Review, as given in Part Third, of this pamphlet. Ministers who "stand firmly by righteousness and truth," and lift up their voices to testify against the sins and iniquities of those in high positions, will have their pay stopped. And every one who is in the employ of the denomination in any capacity, and takes the side of right, will be treated in the same manner. and their "prosperity" will suffer in consequence. Every one in this little company will have to sacrifice the friendship of many whom they had loved as brethren. In addition to this, they will bring upon their heads the denunciations of many of the leaders * and ministers, and will, in many cases, be expelled from their churches. They will be thrown into great anxiety and distress of mind, on account of these things. But they will carry their point, and come off victorious nevertheless. The control of the denomination will pass out of the hands of unfaithful men who now direct its affairs, and pass into the hands of this small company of true men. We will prove this.

"Those who have trusted to intellect, genius, or talent, will not then [in the shaking time] stand at the head of rank and file. They did not keep pace with the light. Those who have proved themselves unfaithful will not then be entrusted with the flock. In the last solemn work few great men will be engaged. They are self-sufficient, independent of God, and he cannot use them. The Lord has faithful servants, who in the shaking, testing time, will be disclosed to view. There are precious ones, now hidden, who have not bowed the knee to Baal. They have not had the light which has been shining in a concentrated blaze upon you. But, it may be, under a rough and uninviting exterior, the pure brightness of a genuine christian character will be revealed." -T. 31, pp. 76, 77. These new leaders will be reinforced by an army who, like them, came to the front in the extremity of the church. "When trees without fruit are cut down as cumberers of the ground, when multitudes of false brethren are distinguished from the true; then the hidden ones will be revealed to view, and. with hosannas, range under the banner of Christ. Those who have been timid and self-distrustful, will declare themselves openly for Christ and his truth. The most weak and hesitating in the church will be as David— willing to do and to dare. The deeper the night for God's people, the more brilliant the stars. Satan will sorely harrass the faithful, but in the name of Jesus they will come off more than conquerors. Then will the church of Christ appear "fair as the moon, clear as the sun, and terrible as an army with banners."

It will be seen by these passages, that the "shaking" and the "testing" time are spoken of together. The shaking is the agitation arising from causes within the church. While the "testing" is from outside causes. We will now prove these two facts—"I asked the meaning of the shaking I had seen, and was shown, that it would be caused by the straight Testimony called forth by the counsel of the True Witness to the Laodiceans. This will have its effect upon the heart of the receiver and will lead him to exalt the standard, and pour forth the straight truth. Some will not bear this straight Testimony. They will rise up against it, and this is what will cause a shaking among God's people."—Early Writings, pp. 131, 132. "The time is not far distant when the "test" will come to every soul. The Mark of the Beast will be urged upon us." T. 31, p. 77. The first of these quotations proves that the "shaking" arises from causes within the church; while the "test" comes from without. The "shaking" draws the line between the two classes in the church. and the "test" sweeps the chaff—the multitude of false brethren—out. perfecting the work of purification of the church which the shaking had begun. The Shaking immediately precedes and leads into the loud cry and the conflict, as will be seen by reading the chapter on "The Shaking" in Early Writings, which we give at the conclusion of this subject.

COMMENCED.

The Shaking is about to begin in earnest. We have raised the standard, exposed the rotten condition of things in the church, and the waters are beginning to be stirred. In other words, the collision between those who stand firmly by "righteousness and truth," and the rest of the denomination, is about to occur. The challenge is out. The gauntlet is down. We see signs that the challenge will be accepted. Since placing Part Third in the printer's hands, we have read the "proceedings of the Mo Conference," in the Review. Those who took part in those proceedings may be "dead to righteousness," but they are not quite dead to the situation. They seem to sniff the coming battle. They apprehend that this matter may not be confined to Mo.. but may "reach other Conferences" We wish to assure them that their fears are well founded. This matter, beginning in Mo., will spread throughout the world. wherever there are Adventists that abhor criminals and idiots, and believe in "standing firmly by righteousness and truth." We are threatened with being fired upon through the columns of the Review. We shall not object to this. if they should be foolish enough to put themselves on "record" any more. If they do open fire on us with the big Michigan blunderbuss. we hope it will not burst like the little blunderbuss did. that they shot off down here in "poor Missouri." This little one must have burst. for the bullets did not reach the mark aimed at, till we ourself went all through the state. picked up the bullets and carried them to their destination! (The letters Jones sent to the churches in regard to us. with the request that they be read to the churches. had not been read, except in two or three cases—and we got the elders to let us read them, or to read them themselves.) It may be that the blunderbuss did not burst. Perhaps there was not powder—force—enough behind the bullets to drive them through. At any rate we did not like to see such bullets lost, so we assisted them to reach the mark, as above described. It may be seen, from our action in the matter, that we believe in giving Jones a hearing. We don't believe much in gag law. We don't believe in gagging even idiots, though they sometimes gag us. They not only gag our mouth, but they "gag" our stomach, also.

But we have wandered from our subject. We were speaking of the big blunderbuss they are going to shoot at us from Michigan. Now, if they do shoot it, we hope it will not burst. Or, if it should burst, we hope the pieces may not kill them. Because, we expect, we shall want another chance at them before they go "clean dead." We want them to put in a little more powder too, for we do not want to waste our time helping the bullets to get to their destination. Instead of shooting at us with blunderbusses, and running the risk of having them burst, and either hurt, or kill, themselves and bother us to go around and help their bullets reach the mark, we advise that they wake up the "Big Injin"—the G(reat) I. B(e)—the Mighty Chief. Let him put on his Eagle's feathers, and his bear's claws—let him paint the demons on his cheeks that play in his heart—let him summon his braves around him—then, with one hand, brandishing his bloody tomahawk, and with the other, flourishing the reeking scalp of D. M. Canright, let him raise the warwhoop, and rush into the fight. When the fight is over, the query, on every hand, will be

"Where, O where, is he!"

"But the days of the purification of the church are hastening on apace. God will have a people, pure and true. In the mighty sifting soon to take place, we shall be better able to measure the strength of Israel. The signs reveal, that the time is near when the Lord will manifest that his fan is in his hand, and he will thoroughly purge his floor." --T. 30, p. 76. When that has taken place, we shall be able to bid farewell to sin, and crime, and confusion in the church. Then the church will appear without "spot or wrinkle, or any such thing"—then we shall come, in the unity of the faith, unto a perfect man, unto the measure of the stature of the fullness of Christ." Then we shall see flocking to the altars of the church, the saints of God throughout the world—.

"Many as the waves,
But one as the sea "

"Awake, Jerusalem, Awake.
No longer in thy sins lie down.
The garment of Salvation take:
Thy beauty, and thy strength, put on.

Shake off the dust that blinds thy sight,
And hides the promise from thine eyes.
Arise and struggle into light;
The great Deliv'rer calls arise.

Shake off the bands of sad despair.
Zion assert thy liberty.
Look up, thy broken heart prepare,
And God shall set the captive free.

Vessels of Mercy, Sons of grace,
Be purged from every sinful stain.
Be like your Lord, his word embrace,
Nor bear his hallowed name in vain."

We here give the most of the chapter on the Shaking, just as it is found in Early Writings, p. 131, *et seq:*

"I saw some with strong faith, and agonizing cries, pleading with God. Their countenances were pale and marked with deep anxiety, expressive of their internal struggle. Firmness and great earnestness was expressed in their countenances; large drops of perspiration fell from their foreheads. Now and then their faces would light up with the marks of God's approbation, and again the same solemn, earnest, anxious look, would settle upon them.

Evil angels crowded around them, pressing darkness upon them, to shut out Jesus from their view, that their eyes might be drawn to the darkness that surrounded them, and thus they be led to distrust God, and murmur against him. Their only safety was in keeping their eyes directed upward. Angels of God had charge over his people, and as the poisonous atmosphere of evil angels was pressed around these anxious ones, the heavenly angels were continually wafting their wings over them to scatter the thick darkness.

As the praying ones continued their earnest cries, at times, a ray of light from Jesus came to them, to encourage their hearts, and light up their countenances. Some, I saw, did not participate in this work of agonizing and pleading. They seemed indifferent and careless. They were not resisting the darkness around them, and it shut them in like a thick cloud. The angels of God left these, and went to the aid of the earnest, praying ones. I saw angels of God hasten to the assistance of all who were struggling with all their power to resist the evil angels, and trying to help themselves by calling upon God, with perseverance. But his angels left those who made no effort to help themselves, and I lost sight of them.

I asked the meaning of the Shaking I had seen, and was shown that it would be caused by the straight Testimony called forth by the True Witness to the Laodiceans. This will have its effect upon the heart of the receiver, and cause him to exalt the standard and pour forth the straight truth. Some will not bear this straight Testimony. They will rise up against it, and this is what will cause a shaking among Gods people. * * Said the angel—'list ye.' Soon I heard a voice like many musical instruments, all sounding in perfect strains, sweet and harmonious. It surpassed any music I had ever heard, seeming to be full of mercy, compassion and elevating holy joy. It thrilled through my whole being. Said the angel—'look ye.' My attention was then turned to the company who were mightly shaken. I was shown those whom I had before seen weeping and praying with agony of spirit. The company of guardian angels around them had been doubled, and they were clothed with an armor from their head to their feet. They moved in exact order, like a company of soldiers. * They had obtained the victory, and it called forth from them the deepest gratitude, and holy, sacred joy.

The numbers of this company had lessened. Some had been shaken out and left by the way. The careless and indifferent who did not join with those who prized victory and salvation enough to perseveringly plead and agonize for it, did not obtain it, and they were left behind in darkness, and their places were immediately filled by others taking hold of the truth, and coming into the ranks. Evil angels still pressed around them but could have no power over them.

I heard those clothed with the armor speak forth the truth with great power. It had effect. Many had been bound; some wives by their husbands, and some children by their parents. The honest who had been prevented from hearing the truth, now eagerly laid hold upon it. All fear of their relatives was gone, and the truth alone was exalted to them. They had been hungering and thirsting for truth. It was dearer and more precious than life. I asked what had made this great change. An angel answered—'It is the latter rain, the refreshing from the presence of the Lord, the loud cry of the third angel.'

Great power was with these chosen ones. Said the angel—'look ye.' My attention was turned to the wicked or unbelievers. They were all astir. The zeal and power with the people of God had aroused and enraged them. Confusion, confusion, was on every side. I saw measures taken against the company who had the light and power of God. Darkness thickened around them, yet they stood firm, approved unto God and trusting in him. I saw them perplexed; next I heard them crying unto God earnestly. Through the day and night their cry ceased not—'Thy will, O God, be done—they have appointed us unto death, but thine arm can bring salvation.'

* * Soon I heard the voice of God which shook the heavens and the earth. There was a mighty earthquake. Buildings were shaken down on every side. I then heard a triumphant shout of victory, loud, musical and clear. I looked upon the company who, a short time before, were in such distress and bondage Their captivity was turned. A glorious light rested upon them. How beautiful they then looked. All marks of care and weariness were gone, and health and beauty were seen in every countenance. Their enemies around them fell like dead men; they could not endure the light that shone upon the delivered, holy ones. This light and glory remained upon them until Jesus was seen in the clouds of heaven, and the faithful, tried company were changed in a moment, in the twinkling of an eye, from glory to glory. And the graves were opened, and the saints came forth, clothed with immortality, crying— 'Victory over death and the grave,' and together with the living saints they were caught up to meet their Lord in the air, while rich, musical shouts of 'glory' and 'victory' were upon every immortal tongue.''

PART FIFTH.

HEAVEN.

Part Fourth has landed us at a point where it is proper to give a short account of heaven, which we do in this part. The basis of heaven is

THE MATERIAL UNIVERSE.

On this basis we shall proceed in the most simple and direct language, to give a brief account of what we suppose heaven to be.

The material universe is composed of all the material objects contained in it—as suns, moons, planets, comets, etc., with all the various substances composing them—and the inhabitants, whether rational or non-rational, that live upon any of them. These things constitute the material universe. The various forms of matter throughout the universe are essentially the same. Rock, metal, soil, water, air, electricity—these are the elements that lie at the basis of all suns, moons, planets, comets and worlds, as well the earth. The infinite variety of objects in nature is but so many forms of these objects, or of combinations of them. Besides these objects and combinations there are laws, called the laws of nature. These laws acting through these objects and combinations produce effects, as light, heat, life motion. These primary effects become causes in their turn and produce secondary effects, as thought, feeling, force. These again become causes, and as a result, we have knowledge and action, and these result in the endless inventions and productions of men, angels, and other rational inhabitants of the universe. These elements are

INDESTRUCTIBLE.

We have roughly summed these elements up in rock, metal, soil, water, air and electricity. We have not spoken scientifically, of course. As some of these objects are not simple and original elements. But as the original elements are embraced in the make up of these, we have "roughed them off" in this manner. When we say they are indestructible, we mean the original elements embraced in them. These cannot be destroyed by any power less than that of him who created them. The laws, also, that relate to them are unchangeable, and indestructible, except at his pleasure who established them. These being facts, it would also be true, that the various primary and secondary, and all resulting effects, must be invariable and unceasing. Here we get a view of the

STABILITY

of the universe. This stability is contingent only on one fact; and that is, the will of Him who made all things. If to-day were the first day in the history of the universe, there would be indications on the "face of things" that their existence was not intended to be transient. The very existence of such a universe is a prophecy of its permanency. But this is not the first day of its existence. It has already existed many days. Every day since the first, only strengthens the probability that it is to stand forever. It is pretty safe to settle down to the conclusion, that the universe has "come to stay;" and that

IMMORTALITY,

not only of the soul, but of the body, and of nature, and the universe is a fact. The only case in which we would have ground to rationally suppose that immortality would be suspended, or done away, would be, where some disarrangement of the established order should take place. In that case we could not have the same ground, as before, on which to rest our belief in the immortality of the universe, or that part of it where the disarrangement occurred. It would be thoroughly rational to suppose, that the Creator would, at this point, exercise his reserved prerogative, and eliminate the disarranging cause. And if, in his wisdom, he saw, that it would be better, in the long run, not to cast out the disarranging cause at once, we think it is not unrational to suppose, that immortality and the benefits of it would be suspended until the ejection of the disturbing agent, or cause, at least. But, with this exception, we cannot think of a single reason which would render it likely that the state of things would cease. It becomes almost a certainty that it will not permanently cease, when we reflect, that the whole arrangement seems to have been made with reference to the

HAPPINESS

of living creatures, and intelligent beings. All the elements, even for the enjoyment of animal life, exist. Plains to roam over, and forests to hide in. Streams to drink from, and verdure to feed upon. Sunlight to warm them, and ever present atmosphere to breathe. Skies in which birds may soar and sing, and oceans for fishes. While every object is, in some way, designed to add to the pleasure of mere existence.

But when we come to intelligent beings—to man, for instance—we see more strikingly than ever, that happiness is designed for them. Even his animal life is to be of a higher order. His very form is in token of this. While his finer organization bespeaks a higher pleasure. Then there are many pleasures exclusively theirs. One of the first and greatest of which is,

INTELLIGENT INTERCOURSE

with his fellows. In this intercourse, each one relates to the other, or others, his experience in whatever he may have been concerned, and lays open his plans an l hopes for the future, and asks the opinion an l counsel of his fellows on the matters brought forward for conversation. The themes of conversation from time to time, will be as varied as the experience and knowledge of each, and all the individuals, engaged, and will be as brilliant as their minds are polished, and as agreeable as their feelings are refined and genial. But in addition to this, there will be another source of pleasure found in the great variety of

AVOCATIONS.

A universe—or even a single world—cannot be suitably carried on without much activity, iu various ways. And this will lead to an endless variety of callings; giving to every one the opportunity of suiting both his talents and his tastes, in the choice he would be privileged to make among them. This point being gained, and this pleasure seized, the next source of happiness would be,

TO MASTER

the calling chosen. This would call forth all the powers, and with immortality abiding in, and rousing those powers, what might such a one not hope to achieve. This would bring him to another fountain. from which to fill his cup afresh, and drink of unalloyed pleasure. He would now be able to realize that most deep-seated longing of the heart of an intelligent being, viz.:

TO BE GREAT.

Great in powers and in achievements. He can now know the pleasure of being great in both respects. It is a greatness that may become greater yet. From the summit of solid attainments, he may survey the field of endless, future conquests, and so, enjoyment of the present. blended with hope of the future, and memory of the past renders him a happy being. Yet his happiness is not complete, for he now longs to find a being that

IS GREATER

than he. He finds some who have excelled him in the development of their powers, and in their achievements, but this does not satisfy him. He would like—his soul longs—to find a being whose powers embrace all intellect, and all soul, and whose achievements are unmeasurable. He would like to find Him who made the universs, if he could be found. He finds Him. Finds Him illimitably great. He falls at his feet. He wonders. He admires. He adores. He loves, and of course, evermore obeys. He is now in full possession of happiness. There is not an unsatisfied longing in his heart. We said awhile ago, that the desire to be great was the most deeply seated longing in the heart of an intelligent being. But we were mistaken. The desire to find one greater than ourselves—the desire to find the one, Supremely Great, lies deeper still. It lies at the bottom of the depths of the soul. Extend this state of things throughout the universe. and each inhabited world becomes a heaven. and the universe itself is the "heaven of heavens." That particular world where Go l dwells, and where the seat of his government is, is heaven "par

excellence." This is the heaven so much talke l about, and which the saints of
God are to be permitted to visit, at the Second Coming of Christ.

Who, who would live alway—away from his God,
Away from you heaven, that blissful abode,
Where rivers of pleasure flow bright o'er the plains,
And the noon-tide of glory eternally reigns.

There saints of all ages in harmony meet,
Their Savior and brethren transported to greet,
While anthems of pleasure unceasingly roll,
And the smile of the Lord is the feast of the soul.

PART SIXTH.

HELL.

We have quit apologizing for adding new parts to this pamphlet. If all
we have said in the preceding parts be true. a brief discussion of "Hell" is in
order. And we begin by giving an account of the great fires of Northern Michigan and Wisconsin, which transpired in 1871. We quote the language of the
Detroit Free Press, as follows:—

"Fires had been burning in Sanilac, Huron, and Tuscola counties, but no
one apprehended any danger. Farmers had set fire to slashings to clear the
ground for fall wheat. but this happens every fall, and the fact that not a drop
of water had fallen in from fifty to seventy days was not considered, by those
who saw the smoke clouds. and replied that there was no danger. There was
danger. Behind that pall of smoke was a greater enemy than an earthquake,
and it had a tornado at its back, and two hundred miles of forest in the front.
From noon until two o'clock a strange terror held the people in its grip; then,
all of a sudden, the heavens took fire, or so it seemed to hundreds. In some lo-
calities it came with a sound of thunder. In others it was preceded by a terrific roaring, as if a tidal wave were sweeping over the country. Almost at the
same moment the flames appeared in every spot over a district of country thirty
miles broad by one hundred in length.

At Richmondville, ten miles above Sanilac, 150 people had comfortable
homes, stacks of hay and grain, teams, cows, pigs, sheep, and no fear of the
fire which they knew was burning a mile away. At two o'clock the flames
rushed out of the woods, leaped the fences, ran across the bare fields, and swal-
lowed every house but two, and roasted a dozen people. It is hardly forty rods
to the beach of the lake, and yet many people had no time to reach the water.
Others reached it with clothing on fire, and faces and hands blistered. The
houses did not burn singly, but billows of flames seized them all at once, and
reduced them to nothing in ten minutes.

"I saw many and many a spot where the billows of fire jumped a clean
half mile out of the forest to clutch a house or barn. The Thornton family
were wiped out with the exception of a boy. Thornton had hitched up the
team to drive the family to a place of safety. but when he saw they were all
surrounded by the flames. he unhitched the horses in despair. Before they
could be unharnessed, they bolted in different directions. and the old man became so confused that he ran directly towards a big slashing. which was then a
perfect mass of flames. and dropped and died with his head toward it.

"Meantime the mother and children had taken refuge in the root house.

This was a structure mostly sunk in the ground, and the roof well covered with earth. Here they were all right for a time, but when the father failed to join them one of the sons went out to see what caused the delay. He was hardly out of the place before the door through which he had passed was in flames. In this emergency he ran to a dry creek, and by lying on his face and keeping his mouth to the ground he lived through it.

"I talked with a woman who lived neighoor to Thorntons, and who escaped by fleeing to a field of plowed ground. This was only a few rods from the root house, and she said it was fully an hour before the screams and shrieks, and groans, from the people inside grew quiet in death. One by one they were suffocated by heat and smoke, and their bodies presented a most horrible appearance. To one riding through the district it seems miraculous that a single soul escaped. The fire swept through the green trees the same as the dry. It ran through the fields of corn at the rate of twenty miles an hour, and fields of clover were swept as bare as a floor. Dark and gloomy swamps, filled with stagnant water, and the homes for years of wild cats, bears and snakes, were struck and shriveled and burnt almost in a flash. Over the parched meadows the flames ran faster than a horse could gallop. Horses did gallop before them, but were overtaken and left roasting on the ground. It seemed as if every hope and avenue of escape was cut off, and yet hundreds of lives were spared. People spent ten to twenty hours in ditches and ponds, or in fields under wet blankets, having their hair singed, their limbs blistered, and their clothing burned off piece by piece. In dozens of cases the first flames spared houses and farms, but after seeming to have passed on for miles, suddenly circled back and made a clean sweep of everything. Unless one rides over the burnt district he cannot believe the eccentricities of a forest fire. In the great swamps, between Sanilac and Sandusky, it burned everything to the roots for a mile in breadth. Then it left patches from ten feet to ten rods wide. Then again it struck in and burned lanes hardly twenty feet wide, leaving half a mile of fuel on either side. In timber it seemed to strike the green trees harder than the dry ones. It was like a great serpent making its way across the country. It would run within three feet of a wheat stack, and then glide away to lick up a house. It would burn a stack and spare a barn ten feet off.

"People felt the heat while the fire was yet miles away. It withered the leaves of trees standing two miles from the path of the fiery serpent. The very earth took fire in hundreds of places, and blazed up as if the fire were feasting on cordwood. The stoutest log buildings stood up only a few minutes. The fire seemed to catch them at every corner at once, and after a whirl and a roar nothing would be left. Seven miles off the beach, at Forester, sailors found the heat uncomfortable. Where some houses and barns were burned, we could not find even a blackened stick. Every log, beam and board was reduced to fine ashes.

"Seven miles back from the lake at Forester, a farmer gathered up fifteen persons in his wagon, and started for the beach. The fire was close behind them as they started—so close that the dresses of some of the women and children were on fire from the sparks. It was seven miles up hill and down, with corduroy ruts and roots, and the horses needed no whip to urge them into a mad run. As the wagon started the tire of one hind wheel rolled off. They could not stop for it, and yet, even on a good road, the wheel would have crushed down in going twenty rods without it. It is an actual fact that the horses pushed over that seven miles of rough road at a wild run, and the wheel stood firm. A delay of five minutes at any point of the road would have given fifteen more victims to the flames which followed on behind. I saw the wagon at the lake. And I saw the tire seven miles away on the roadside.

"The people who sought the beach had still to endure much of the heat and all of the smoke. Wading up to their shoulders, they were safe from the flames, but sparks and cinders fell like a snow-storm, and the smoke was suffocating. The birds not caught in the woods, were carried out to sea and drowned, and the waves have washed thousands of them ashore. Squirrels, rabbits, and such small animals, stood no show at all, but deer and bear sought the beach and the company of human beings. In one case a man leaped from a bluff into the lake, and found himself close behind a large bear. They remained in company under the bank all night and the bear seemed as humble as a dog. In another instance two of the animals came out of the forest and stood close to a well, from which a farmer was drawing water to dash over his house, and they were with him for two hours before they deemed it prudent to jog along. Deer came out and sought the companionship of cattle and horses, and paid no attention to persons rushing past them."

A correspondent of the Milwaukee Sentinel describes the fires in Wisconsin as follows:

"Oh God! what a scene met my gaze on every side. Here came the crisis of the storm; here the fiery elements, controlled by a tornado and a whirlwind, made war on human hopes, hearts, and life. The half has not been told, nor ever can be.

"The phenomena and results of this storm were mysteriously strange. In some places the forest trees lay in every imaginable position, while in others they were carried into windrows. They were mere sticks in the hands of a great power, slashing and whipping the earth, and then made fuel for the work of death. The fields, woods, barns, houses and even the air, were on fire, while large balls of fire were revolving and bursting in every direction, igniting every thing they came in contact with ; and the whole of this devouring element was driven before a tornado at the rate of a mile a minute. There can be little doubt that the air, strongly charged with electricity, helped on the work of destruction and death. Mr. Kirby says, he saw large balls of fire in the air, and when they came in contact with anything, they would bound thirty or forty rods away. Others testify that they saw large clouds of fire burst into fragments, and in some instances great tongues of fire, like lightning, would issue from the dark clouds and light upon the buildings. Pennies were melted in the pockets of persons who were but little burned. A small bell upon an engine, and a new stove, standing from twenty to forty feet from any building were melted.

"Many thought that the 'great day of his wrath' had come. And why should they not? If persons who visit the ruins since the fire are forced to think that God hid his face in wrath, and sent forth his thunderbolts of destruction; nay, that he gave the very fiends of hell the right and power to shake the place and burn it up, what must have been feelings of those who passed through the fiery ordeal?"

The Detroit Post spoke of the same fires in the following terms:

"Those who were exposed to the terrible tornado during which Chicago, Peshtigo, Manistee, White Rock, and other towns on Lake Michigan and Huron, were burned, testify nearly unanimously that, the air seemed to be on fire. These words are almost invariably used in describing the phenomena. The

fire did not spread gradually from tree to tree, and house to house, but a rgreat
sheet of flame, overcoming them like the clouds, and moving with the rapidity
of a hurricane, rushed upon them without warning. It surrounded them.
The atmosphere seemed filled with fire. Many people who inhaled the hot air
fell dead. Corpses were found without a trace of fire upon them,
or even upon the clothes which still covered them. There were frequent-
ly no marks of fire among the adjacent trees and fences. Many were killed in
compact masses as if by a blast of death. They were found huddled together
away from trees and buildings. Fish were killed in the streams by the intense
heat. Many of these people believed that the last day had come; as well they
might. The roaring of the whirlwind which preceded the blaze sounded
enough like the last trump to suggest a prelude to the final catastrophe. The
black midnight sky suddenly burst into flame."

We now give a short account of the burning of Chicago. The account is
taken from the Detroit Post and runs as follows:

"A strong wind was blowing at that time, and yet the flames seemed to go into all directions, like an expanding scythe, mowing great and increasing swaths
with frightful rapidity. We could think of nothing else but hell.
The flames were in some places like huge waves, dashing to and fro,
leaping up and down, turning and twisting and pouring,—now and
then—a great column of smoke and blaze hundreds of feet into the
air, like a solid perpendicular shaft of molten metal. In other places it would
dart out long streaks, like mammoth anacondas, with hissing, fiery tongues;
then these serpentine shapes would swoop down over the blazing path into the
yet unburned buildings, which seemed pierced and kindled instantaneously.
There were also billows of flame that rolled along like water, submerging everything in their course. There was a terrible fascination in gazing upon the
scene.

"It was unearthly, hideous, terrific. Our eyes seemed riveted so that we
could not withdraw them. There were miles of fire, mountains of flame,
waves of light, flashes, clouds, brilliant scintillations. With the aid of glass-
es we could see the streets thronged with people flying for their lives. Close to
their heels in hot pursuit, came the belching, roaring, crackling flames. In
some places they actually advanced as fast as men could run. The most awful
of all was the thunderous roar that seemed to roll upward and outward from
the center of the huge holocaust."

D. L. Moody, speaking of this fire, says: As the flames rolled down our
streets, destroying everything in their onward march, I saw the great and honorable, the learned and wise, fleeing before the fire with the beggar, und the
thief, and the harlot. All were alike. As the flames swept over the city it
was like the judgment day. Neither the mayor, nor the mighty men, nor the
wise men could stop the flames."

One more quotation and we conclude our description of hell:

"Rome was an ocean of flame. Height and depth were covered with red
surges, that rolled before the blast like an endless tide. The billows burst up
the sides of the hills, which they turned into instant volcanoes, exploding vol-
umes of smoke and fire; then plunged into the depths in a hundred glowing
cataracts, then climbed and consumed again. The distant sound of the city, in
her convulsion, went to the soul. The air was filled with the steady roar of the
advancing flame, the crash of falling houses, and the hideous outcry of the
myriads, flying through the streets, or surrounded and perishing in the conflagration.

"All was clamor, violent struggle and helpless death. Men and women of the highest rank were on foot, trampled by the rabble, that had then lost all respect for condition. One dense mass of miserable life, irresistible from its weight, crushed by the narrow streets, and scorched by the flames over their heads, rolled through the gates like an endless stream of black lava. The fire had originally broken out on the Palatine, and hot smoke that wrapped, and half blinded us hung thick as night upon the wrecks of pavilions and palaces; but the dexterity and knowledge of my inexplicable guide carried us on. It was vain that I insisted on knowing the purpose of this terrible traverse. He pressed his hand upon his heart in reassurance of his fidelity, and still spurred on. We now passed under the shade of an immense range of lofty buildings, whose gloomy and solid strength seemed to void defiance to chance and time.

"A sudden yell appalled me. A ring of fire swept round its summit : burning cordage, sheets of canvas, and a shower of all things combustible, flew into the air above our heads. An uproar followed, unlike all that I had ever heard, a hideous mixture of howls, shrieks, and groans. The flames rolled down the narrow street before us, and made the passage next to impossible. While we hesitated, a huge fragment of the building heaved as if in an earthquake, and fortunately for us, fell inward. The whole scene of terror was then open. The great amphitheatre of Statilius Taurus had caught fire; the stage with its inflamable furniture, was intensely blazing below. The flames were wheeling up, circle after circle, through the seventy thousand seats that rose from the ground to the roof. I stood in unspeakable awe and wonder on the side of this colossal cavern, this mighty temple of the city of fire. At length a descending blast cleared away the smoke that covered the arena. The cause of those horrid cries was now visible. The wild beasts kept for the games had broken from their dens. Maddened by fright and pain, lions, tigers, panthers, wolves, whole herds of the monsters of India and Africa, were inclosed in an impassable barrier of fire. They bounded, they fought, they screamed, they tore; they ran howling round and round the circle; they made desperate leaps upward through the blaze; they were flung back, and fell only to fasten their fangs in one another; and, with their parching jaws bathed in blood, to die raging.

"I looked anxiously to see whether any human being was involved in this fearful catastrophe. To my great relief, I could see none. The keepers and attendants had obviously escaped. As I expressed my gladness, I was startled by a loud cry from my guide, the first sound that I had heard him utter. He pointed to the opposite side of the amphitheater. There indeed sat an object of melancholy interest; a man who had been either unable to escape, or had determined to die. Escape was now impossible. He sat in desperate calmness on his funeral pile. He was a gigantic Ethiopean slave, entirely naked. He had chosen his place, as if in mockery, on the imperial throne; the fire was above him and around him, and under the canopy; he gazed, without the movement of a muscle, on the combat of the wild beasts below; a solitary sovereign with the whole tremendous game played for himself, and inaccessible to the power of man."

The scenes described in these quotations are hells, on a small scale. Extend them until the whole earth, with every living object, is involved, and you will have the last great hell.

In other words, the last great hell is simply the

in this conflagration, Satan and fallen angels, and lost men disappear, and in their disappearance, the cause of the sins and miseries of the world vanish. While. from the ashes of this great fire—like the bird of Eastern legend—rises the new, and uncursed earth.

PART SEVENTH.

THE MISSOURI CONFERENCE.

As this Conference is destined to furnish a full quota of victims to the last devouring flames, we give it the benefit of this part of our pamphlet. We begin by making some quotations from the "Proceedings" of the last session. The second paragraph has this:

"The president made a verbal report of the work done in the Conference during the past year, calling attention to questions of interest coming up for consideration at this session."

After the "whereases" and the "resolutions," we find this:

"The president addressed the delegates on the subject of dealing with those who are headstrong, or inclined to pursue an independent course, also those who have been disfellowshipped."

A little further on we find the following:—

"The committee appointed to suggest a plan for dealing with unruly members. reported in substance as follows: 'That we would not advise the publication of their course through the Review, unless their work threatens to become an injury to other conferences; but that we heartily indorse the course taken by the president of this conference, in warning our churches against such persons, to be wise and commendable, and that it is the sense of this conference that all similar cases be treated in like manner." From this it appears that the Mo. Conference is made of the same "stuff" that Jones is. They sanction the letter he sent out in regard to us as "wise and commendable." In the estimation of this conference it is "wise and commendable" to charge a man with having committed a "crime" when he has committed none, but has obeyed the laws of his state. and l of the world; and of God. and has performed an act, every element of which was not only not criminal, but was demanded by every claim of duty and affection.

QUERY:—Was the Mo. Conference a conclave of devils, or a herd of idiots? How fast is this conference revealing its own rottenness. If the same state of things exists elsewhere the "Shaking" has not begun any too soon. We know that the Big Butler sanctions these crimes of Jones, and we shall not be surprised to find the bulk of every conference equally putrid.

We fail to find the names of the committee who made the delectable report above quoted. We should be glad to know who they were.

After the conference had unloaded itself as above. it "proceeded," among other things, to give "Colporter's license to D. T. Shireman." This matter demands a little notice. What is meant by "colporter's license?" We suppose it must be license to be a "colporter." But what is a colporter? Here is where the puzzle comes in. We shall have to look at the etymology of this word— colporter—a little. Maybe we can get a clue to its meaning by doing so. Now. this word is evidently composed of two words, or of one word and a prefix. The first part is "col" and the second is "porter." There would be no question, we suppose, (unless the learned Jones would question it.) that this "col" is from "con." In Latin "con" means "together." Changed into "col," it would probably mean "coilect." Then joining the two definitions it would mean, "collect together." So far so good.

We now take up "porter." The task here is not quite so easy. But we do not despair, though we may have to call upon the science of Philology to come to the aid of our etymology. But, to begin the task,—it will not be denied (unless by the learned!) that "porter" is from the Latin, also. It comes from "porto"—"to carry." We will tell how the Latins got it. After the destruction of Troy, Æneas found it lying among the ruins. He picked it up and "carried" it away with him, when, having been

"Driven much by land and sea,
He came at last to Italy."

Now, leaving off the "o" from "porto," we have "port," which is called the "root of the word. Now, when Æneas had safely arrived in Italy, he planted this "root," along with others, in the soil of Italy, and "raised the Latin language. But Æneas and his descendants never forgot the meaning of "port." They soon began to practice what it taught, and one of the first things they "carried" was the "Sabine women," whom they forcibly took and made wives. This proving a profitable instance of "carrying," they concluded they would make "carrying" their national calling. They went to work to "carry" the crowns of kings, and the treasures of all nations, to Rome. until they came to be called the "robbers" of nations.

As to where the Trojans got this word, we can't tell. unless Paris brought it from Greece, when he "carried" off Helen. The Greeks must have brought it along when they "carried" fire from the altars of heaven to be scattered among men. But, however this may be, when the Romans got done with it, and quit the "carrying" business, the Franks got hold of it by some means, and "carried" it into France. This last named nation has been practicing upon it, but have not been so successful as the Romans. It will be remembered that it used to be upon a time that the French thought they would "carry" England across the British Channel. But they did not succeed. Somewhat later, they had had some success in "carrying" off different countries, and they thought they would pick up Russia and do a big job of this kind. But they did not "carry" Russia very far. Russia is there yet. The next enterprise of this kind the French undertook was when they thought they would clandestinely "carry" off Mexico. But, according to the latest maps. Mexico is still a part of North America. They then went back to Europe. and their latest feat in this line was when they were going to "carry" Germany across the Rhine. But they did not succeed. At least, the last Teuton we talked with on the subject said they did not.

Perhaps we are going too fully into the philology of this word. Well, to make a long matter short, somebody has "carried" this "port" over into our country. where it has crept into a lot of our words. The Americans are not so famous for "carrying" as some others have been. Yet they did manage to "carry" a continent off from their mother, and we have heard that they since "carried" off a certain, so-called, "Confederacy."

"Col-port," then. is to "collect together" and "carry" off something. A "colporter" is one who "collects" things "together" and "carries" them off. Here is the clue. we think. to the action of the Mo. Conference in giving colporter's license to D. T. Shireman. For the said Shireman had been engaged in "collecting" our goods and "carrying" them off. In other words, D. T. Shireman had been stealing from us. In the month of February, 1888, he stole from us a carpet, and other things. Now, since the fact of his having done so was known to the Mo. Conference, when it gave him "colporter's" license, are we not obliged to conclude that they have licensed him to "collect" and "carry" off the goods of other people? Or, in other words,—to steal?

Can it be possible that the Mo. Conference intend to insult and outrage the people of Kansas City—or the lowest of them—by asking them to admit this thief into their houses, to read the Bible and pray with them? Or do they consider him just the man for that kind of work. because, having stolen our carpet and put it down in his own parlor. he has such a nice place in which to get down on his knees and pray before going out to pray with the people? You know after he had prayed a long time with his knees on our carpet. such a saintly influence would follow him among the people. and he could "colport" both them and their goods so piously.

In what we have said above. we have spoken as if the whole conference had taken part in these senseless and wicked proceedings. True, no one raised a voice against them. Yet we know there were those there who were opposed to such folly. It was proper to let the dominant spirit show itself fully. which it has done. The corruption of Jones and his backers stands fully revealed. And the time has now come, when every Adventist in the state will have to clear himself of all complicity in these crimes, or become "partakers" of their "sins and iniquities." They must speak out against such doings. before our conference goes wholly to the devil.

We know the means used in order to force some true men to take active part in these wrongs. If C. H. Chaffee and R. S. Donnell can be bought, or forced, to sanction what they know to be wrong and idiotic, we shall be surprised. Who knows but that they "may have come to the throne for such a time." So far as the ministry is concerned, it depends upon these two men to save our conference from irretrievable ruin and disgrace.

A Scene—Such a man as Jones addressing such a crowd as this conference, on the subject of guarding the sacred cause of God in Mo. from injury.

Another Scene—Angels of God who have witnessed the whole history of this world without ever being obliged to take emetics. are now seen relieving their stomachs.

Another Scene—"Plug-ugly" Shireman "colporting" his prayers, and the prayers of the Mo. Conference around among decent people in Kansas City.

Another Scene—"The great army of apostles, the glorious army of holy prophets, and the mighty army of saints and martyrs" turning their faces downward, in their graves. to keep from witnessing the last scene.

PART EIGHTH.

SCIENCE AND THE BIBLE.

There is no conflict between Science and the Bible. The science of language does not conflict with it. Nor does the science of Arithmetic, or Algebra, or Geometry, or Astronomy, or Botany, or Zoology, or Geography, or Chemistry, or Physics. These sciences and the Bible are in blissful harmony and are likely to remain so. We don't know of any other sciences, except such as constitute subdivisions of the above, and are included in them.

But, says one, there is Geology, and there is Biology—surely, they are sciences, and surely they conflict with the Bible. We do not consider them sciences, in the full sense of that word. And it is too soon to say they conflict with the Bible. When they have become sciences, in the full sense, then we can tell whether such a conflict will exist. Great and noble efforts have been, and still are being, made to create the science of Geology. These efforts, with others yet to be made, will eventuate in such a science.

It is the same with Biology. Such a science is "coming." But let's wait until it gets here. When Geological and Biological studies have given us sciences, the questions which—as yet they have only raised, will be settled, and like everything else that science settles, will be settled to the satisfaction of everybody. Every science unanswerably demonstrates its propositions. Anything short of this is not science.

As to how these Geological and Biological studies will terminate—whether they will finally prove this proposition, or that—we think it is too soon to anticipate. Let students and scientists push their inquiries wherever they may lead, in order to discover the truth, whatever it may be. But let conclusions be scientifically proven, before they are accepted as truth, either by the students themselves, or the rest of the world. Whatever the ultimate conclusion may be, on special points, it never can be scientifically demonstrated that belief in God is unrational. For every step of a scientific argument demonstrates afresh, the presence in nature, at its origin, of a transcendent "mind," and of a power commensurate with it. The more science we have, the more evidence we have of a great "mind" at the bottom of things. And when a great "mind" is proven to have existed, at the same time and place, there must have been a great "person." A mind without a person is incomprehensible, and unrational. The mind that is revealed in one science is the same that is revealed in every other. For there is no conflict between the sciences, or any two of them. The laws of the highest heaven, so far as revealed by Astronomy, are in perfect harmony with every law of nature in this world. This shows that there is but one mind at the bottom of the universe, and one only person possessing that mind. "There is one God and none other"—is a thoroughly rational, and even scientific proposition

We now venture the statement, that the mind that is revealed in the sciences is the same that is revealed in the Bible. In the first place, as already stated, there is no conflict between any existing science and the Bible. There is, thus, a strong proof that the sciences and the Bible are the product of the same mind, and a strong presumption, that when Geology and Biology, become sciences they will not contradict it. Is it objected that the mind revealed through the sciences is a mind without character whereas the mind revealed in Bible is pre-eminently possessed of character? Does the fact that science does, or may, not reveal the character of the mind that lies beneath it, prove that that mind has no moral character? No. surely On the other hand, is there not a presumption amounting to certainty, that a mind which is so much governed by law and reason in the realm of science, will be governed in the same manner in its independent and voluntary actions? Now as character is a series of voluntary actions, it is surely rational, that instead of revealing the principles of moral actions through sciences, God would bring them to view in a system of principles adopted to voluntary actions. In other words, God would likely reveal his character through a moral law, or system of moral laws or government. It would, therefore, be unrational to look for these principles in the sciences, or to suppose, that because they were not revealed there, they were not revealed anywhere.

But if we are to look somewhere else—say to the Bible, or some other book, for these laws and principles, how can we tell whether the book alleged to contain them, really did originate from the one sole transcendent mind that pervades science.

If there were no disagreement between this book and the sciences, this would be a presumption in favor of such book. If it had been written by nonscientific men, this presumption would be greatly strengthened. We have already shown that there is no conflict between the Bible and any known science. And it is well known that the Bible was written largely by men who were not scientists.

But, says one, ought there not to be some evidence besides this, before a race of men should be expected to accept such a book as a genuine revelation· and carry its teachings into effect in their lives? It certainly is rational to suppose that God should look upon the matter in the same light, and should proceed to give special evidence in its favor. Now such evidence would have to be given in a scientific manner, or in some other way. But, if it is given scientifically, it would lose its force, as a special confirmation, and would be classed by men along with other scientific matters. But, if this evidence were given in some other manner, it would constitute

A MIRACLE.

As we have already seen that it is rational to expect special evidence in the premises, and as special evidence cannot be given but by miracles, it is rational to expect miracles, and to believe in them when they are given and properly attested. The Bible miracles fall in here naturally. They are out of the line of Science, and they are such as could have been performed only by that God who had laid the foundations of the world in the laws of nature, and could arrest the operation of those laws, and substitute a miracle, for the time being, in place of their ordinary action.

Such miracles were the Deluge, the Passage of the Red Sea, the humiliation of Nebuchadnezzar, the swallowing and ejecting of Jonah, by a small throated fish, the Resurrection of Christ, and so on through the whole list. And they were all connected with the teaching, or enforcement, or exemplification, or triumph of moral law. It is thought that the resurrection is the most unrational of all miracles. But, on the contrary, is it not the most rational? Is it not rational, in the highest degree, that such a being as Christ should rise from the dead. Sin and imperfection alone are perishable. How rational, then, that a being so free from these, as was Christ, should not long be "holden of death." The resurrection of all good persons is rational, for the good which they practiced is imperishable, and why not they also. The resurrection of the wicked is rational, too. For, right being imperishable, can never release the wicked, until they have been punished as they deserve. If they were not so punished before they died, it is rational to suppose they will be raised from the dead for this purpose. The miracles of the Bible then are thoroughly rational.

ITS TEACHINGS.

These are also in the highest degree rational. It is rational that a man should comply with the moral requirements of the Bible. It is rational that God would provide a way to forgive those who had done wrong, and were anxious to recover themselves from that wrong. And so through the whole list of

Bible teaching. But some one says, there are those immoralities, and cruelties mentioned in the Bible. Yes, but the immoralities belonged to men, and not to God. But why did God have them mentioned in the Bible? We might ask, why did men commit them? We might ask, why do men not only commit such things yet, but why do they—even some who do not believe the Bible —talk about such things, and why do they laugh and roar when they hear unchaste stories. Why are they so intent on reading newspapers filled with such things. Why do they not object to the newspapers, because they contain such things? We suspect that men are not right sincere when they denounce certain things in the Bible, and take such a pleasure in them everywhere else. The Bible takes the world as it found it, and after revealing the state of things in it, goes to work to cure them, as far as can be done. But its denouncers stop short of applying the remedy.

As to the wars that God caused to be waged, is it any worse for God to subdue his enemies, than for the United States to conquer those who rebel against its authority? We think it is in the memory of living men, that the United States government raised and equipped vast armies, and sent them to conquer, or exterminate, those who had recently been our fellow-citizens. And, what is more, our skeptical citizens, not only did not denounce the enterprise as criminal, but actually approved of it, and some of them went along to help conquer, or kill, their recent brethren. We have heard, however, that some of them resigned, before they had killed very many of their former associates.

Thus it is clearly proven that science and the Bible are in harmony, and that they both originated with the "One, only, God" of the universe.

. THE WORLD'S MISTAKE.

We mean the mistake it has made, by substituting theological discussion, and metaphysical speculation, for scientific investigation. We fear that our Augustines and Platos have done us an irreparable injury. If the time and talent employed in the line of these men had been given to the scientific study of nature, where might our world not be, in knowledge and discovery? Also in mental development and power. The belief of the mind in the great truths of the word of God—such as the existence, power and glory of God, and the rewards of the future state—coupled with the practice of the simple and beautiful precepts, found in that word—is the foundation that God himself has laid, for an endless and unlimited development of the powers of the mind, and of an endless succession of discoveries in the realm of nature, or science. The future world alone, can retrieve the mistakes of this one, and realize that glory and happiness, which a true religion, joined with a true science are designed to produce.

PART NINTH.

RELIGION AND AMUSEMENTS.

These should go hand in hand. The church is designed to lay the homage of the world at the feet of its Maker. Worship is the exercise of the highest and noblest faculties of the mind, and the practice of it has an enlarging and elevating effect on all the other powers. But then there are

OTHER POWERS.

And these must be exercised also. There are the strictly intellectual faculties, which must be cultivated, by the study of the word of God and Science.

The practical powers are to be train ed by every day grappling with the affairs of life. Then there are the faculties that demand exercise at a time when the foregoing should be relaxed. Here the various amusements of life come in, such as "chit chat," mirthful, or witty, conversation, games, parties, concerts, theaters and shows.

If it be objected that there are evils connected with some of these, we reply that if our pamphlet is true, there are also evils in some churches, and especially in the Adventist church. There are none of these things that are evil in themselves. If the whole mass of our population would unite in worship, at the feet of the great Creator, on suitable occasions, and on other occasions, unite freely in all these amusements, what a different world we should have. We would not have the church afflicted with that "I am holier than thou" spirit, nor would small, or even large, preachers be denouncing "stars" much brighter, and often better than themselves, nor would these "stars" evade the church people in disgust. When the menagerie or circus comes around how much better for both preacher and people to attend, than to have matters as they are?

Is it said that these things need reforming? Please tell us how they can be reformed, if not by bringing about just such a state of things as we have described. In this way the reformation would be mutual. The church would reform the theater, and the show, and the theater and show would reform the church.

Games and social plays should be engaged in by all—if for no other purpose, that the children and youth may be rendered happy in their own homes. With such a state of things in regard to amusements, how long would it take for every "improper" place and thing to disappear? They would soon vanish. And a general and unspeakable happiness would take the place of the divisions and miseries, that now afflict society. How long, O Lord, how long does our poor world intend to mutilate and murder itself? A pure worship, a true science, and universal amusements, are—taken together—a happy world, and a world upon whom the smiles of God will rest, while eternity will witness and record its mighty growth.

We are aware that our views on this subject will appear radical, and even revolutionary, to many. But we think a revolution in these matters, is just what the world needs. The effort to transplant these amusements, from their proper place, into the church, can only end in the ruin of the church. Not because the amusements are wrong, but because everything should be kept in its own place. The mission of the church is the highest on earth. That mission is to lay the homage of a grateful and adoring world at the feet of its Creator. And, to this end the church should have a great and eloquent ministry. But when the church goes into the business of making amusements. She has abandoned the "throne," and resigned her scepter over the souls of men.

PART TENTH.

RELIGION AND COMPULSION.

God tolerates the savages, the Brahmins, the Buddhists, the Mohammedans, the Catholics and the Protestants. He tolerates the pagans, the heathen, and the rest of the world. But the world does not tolerate. Cain did not tolerate Abel. Nebuchadnezzar would not tolerate any who did not worship his

"Image." Antiochus did not tolerate the Jews. The Romans did not tolerate the Christians, neither did the Roman Catholics. And the Protestant world now proposes to follow in their wake, and cease to tolerate those who do not keep Sunday. It is proposed to "compel" a universal observance of this day. This, if successful, will result in another extinction of mind, and its greatest achievements, and in the full restoration of the Dark Ages, if time should continue a few centuries. This work is encouraged, that popes, prelates, priests, and apostate preachers, may again get control of the world, and rule it to gratify their lust of power, and their other lusts.

PART ELEVENTH.

CHRISTIANITY AND OTHER RELIGIONS.

It is well known that many of the best principles of Christianity are also found in the Asiatic religions. It has generally been insisted upon, by believers in Christianity, that those religions had derived these principles from the Bible, either directly, or indirectly. We think this is a serious mistake. Our belief is, that the races where those principles are found, have preserved them from the origin of the race, and that they are entitled to great credit for having done so. Compare their course with that of those who have had what they believe to be a "revealed" religion, and how do the latter stand? Why, the fact is, the Jews who were the first to receive a revelation, apostatized from it, and the so-called Christian world have done about as badly. A large proportion of the teachings contained in the Bible are cast away, by both Jew and Christian, and, in their place the errors of the heathen are held to. Yet the Christian boasts of his superiority to the heathen. We fear the so-called heathen have the better of him in the matter.

PART TWELFTH.

THE LOUD CRY REJECTED.

The Loud Cry has been rejected, by G. I. Butler and his confreres. About three years ago, we began writing up the subject, for the Review. Our first article was a brief sketch of the history of God's people, from Eden down to Rev. 18. In our second article, we described Satan's conquest of the world, and how it is now mustered for the great conflict to arise when the work of Rev. 18 begins. In one or two other articles, we presented the Law of God, which is to be the "bone of contention" in that conflict. Mr. Butler, at this point, ordered the Review to print no more of our articles, although he pronounced them the "best that had ever appeared in the Review." Being shut out of the Review, wa published our book entitled, "Sunday," etc. To gratify Butler, the Gen. Con. of 1886 refused to allow us to advertise the book in the Review, and sell it among our people. We say the Gen. Con. We mean a small part of that body, for there were only a few votes cast. In reference to that book, it is perfectly proper to say, that it contains the principles of the Loud Cry, and that, if Butler had written it, he would have thought it the achievement of his life, while he would have been "lauded to the sky," by his worshippers, and the Gen. Con. would have given both him, and the book, a great "send off."

Our next experience was in Mo. Jones wrote us to come to Kingsville and attend the quarterly meeting in July, 1887. We went, and, at his request, spoke on Rev. 18. He pronounced the discourse evidently the correct way of handling the subject, and said it was the "best address he had ever heard on the fall of Babylon."

Next, we mention our experience in K. C. We asked Shireman for the privilege of addressing the church, one Sabbath. We spoke on Rev. 18, and had a most excellent social meeting after the discourse. We requested that a vote of the church be taken as to whether, or not, we could have the privilege, for a few Sabbaths, to take up that chapter and open it out fully. But Shireman refused to take the vote of the church, and said they would see to it at some "future time." That time has not yet arrived.

In the month of April, 1888, we went to Battle Creek, humiliated ourself in the very dust to Butler, to make a last appeal to him to do justice in the matter. But he refused to even converse, or pray with us. We offered him the manuscript of "The Fall of Babylon," as it is in the first part of this pamphlet, and he refused to read it. We afterwards sent it to him through the mail. Whether he read it, we know not. But whether he did, or did not, he is equally guilty of ignoring and rejecting it. The Testimonies that describe the fall of many of the present leaders, say their fall was because "they did not keep peace with the light."—Test. 31, p. 76. There was no light to come but that of the Loud Cry, when this was written. It can be no light but that of the Loud Cry, that is referred to. Butler has rejected this. So has Jones. And they will cause nearly the whole denomination to reject it. Mrs. White told Butler, in the Testimony to him that we have elsewhere quoted, that he would, in some great crisis of the work, probably, pursue a course that would prove "disastrous to the cause, and fatal to his own soul." This Testimony is now fulfilled. The cause is nearly ruined, as will be soon made manifest, and Butler is a doomed man.

PART THIRTEENTH.

FINAL CONCLUSION.

We have, at last, arrived at the conclusion of this pamphlet. A few remarks, on a few more topics, are proper.

ELDER JAMES WHITE.

This noble man fell at his post, crushed beneath a load of burdens that Butler had a full share in throwing upon him. He used to say that Butler and Canright gave him more trouble than all the rest of the preachers." Canright is gone. He went out like a man. Butler will go out like a dog. The memory of Elder White is sacred to every Adventist. He laid the foundations of the work of God like a master workman. He watched the structure rise with an honorable pride, and trembled only when he contemplated its fate, when it should fall into incompetent hands. His work is done. He "fought the good fight," he "kept the faith." "Henceforth, there is laid up for him a crown of righteousness which the Lord the righteous judge will give him at that day." "Peace to his ashes."

"Asleep in Jesus, soon to rise,
When the last trump shall rend the skies."

MRS. ELLEN G. WHITE.

Faithful woman. She has done a good work. "She hath excelled all the daughters of Zion." Her commission will be returned to the hands that gave it, to receive, in exchange, a crown that will never fade. To her it will be said, "Well done, thou good and faithful servant."

If any should look to her to speak in regard to the present "crisis," we think they will look in vain. Has she not spoken of it freely in her books, and in the Review? If we cannot depend upon her written language, how could we upon what she might say? We are willing, however, to have her speak. We have been urging Butler and Jones to appeal to her, in reference to our charges against them. We still urge them to. We have no acquaintance with her, never having seen her, in our life.

THE LITTLE COMPANY.

To the little company of faithful brethren and sisters, we say, do not be alarmed when waves of opposition rise "tumultuous and high" about you. You are sure of victory. The music, so sweet and thrilling. described in the chapter on the "Shaking," as given in this pamphlet, will be made by you, when you have obtained the "victory," and realize that the church is to be renovated indeed, and become a "glorious church, not having spot, or wrinkle, or any such thing."

"No more shall foes unclean invade,
  Or fill thy hallowed walls with dread."

Soldiers of Christ—arise,
  And put your armor on—
Strong in the strength which God supplies,
  Through his eternal son.

Put all the armor on.
  Like valiant soldiers stand.
Let all your loins be girt with truth,
  Waiting your Lord's command.

O, watch, and fight and pray.
  The battle ne'er give o'er.
Renew it boldly, every day.
  And help divine implore.

This pamphlet reunites the severed "cable" spoken of, by Mrs. White, in a former quotation. It restores to the ship of Zion the lost "chart and compass," and points the drifting bark back to the North Star. It lays hold of the helm, with a firm hand. to turn her again into her heavenward course.

On Time's tempestuous ocean wide,
  A gallant ship set sail.
And out into the raging deep,
  She stood before the gale.

Long was to be her voyage—the time,
  Six thousand years almost,
'Ere she would make the highland heights,
  Along the heavenly coast.

Oft' tempests have assailed her round,
  And stormy winds rose high.
And dark have been the mountain waves,
  That bore her to the sky.

Long, long, she has been out and now
  She nears her haven home.
A beacon light hangs o'er her bow,
  And bids her thither come.

ADIEU.

We shall be harshly judged, and roughly handled, on account of the contents of this book. But there is not a word in it that has been written, either in anger or malice. We have dealt out only such rebukes as the case appeared to us to imperatively demand. We are not seeking for office either. There is not an office in the denomination that we will ever accept. We shall find something to do, in the renovated church, without submitting to the trammels and restraints of a church, or conference, office.

We had supposed that we were writing a book for the perusal of Adventists exclusively. But we now discover that it is also meant for the "rest of mankind." Whoever reads it, will find the truth. The condition of the religious world—including Adventists—is truly stated. At the same time, the foundations and character of the great work to be done, soon, in fulfillment of the first part of Rev. 18, are brought to view, as we suppose. And last, but not least, Butler is held up to the scorn of a world before which he has "posing" as an object of worship. While Jones, and a "large majority" of the preachers and people of the Adventist church, are shown to be as unsanctified a herd of cattle as were ever "corraled." As we have shown, there are "clean" cattle among them, but they are to be pitied.

If any Missouri Adventist should see Jones, would he not have the kindness, to ask him to "please read" "this book to the church." If some one should see Butler, the Great, will he not be kind enough to "let him hear" what has transpired, and request him not to be "perplexed," for the "chickens are only coming home to roost." Tell him not to get "misanthropic," and go about trying to kill somebody. We advised him, years ago, to quit killing men, and go to killing cats. In this last employment, he would find use for all his muscular power—(we have understood that cats are hard to kill. It might require a big man to kill even a little cat.) This calling would also, be suited to his mental and moral faculties, and to his refined tastes, as well. Good Bye, Big Beater. We expect to call again, after you have returned this call of ours. Call on us soon.

www.ingramcontent.com/pod-product-compliance
Lightning Source LLC
Chambersburg PA
CBHW031758090426
42739CB00008B/1070